myra alperson

dim sum bagels and grits

A Sourcebook for Multicultural Families

Farrar, Straus and Giroux
New York

Farrar, Straus and Giroux
19 Union Square West, New York 10003

Distributed in Canada by Douglas & McIntyre Ltd.
Printed in the United States of America
First edition, 2001
5 7 9 10 8 6 4

Library of Congress Cataloging-in-Publication Data

Alperson, Myra.
Dim sum, bagels, and grits : a sourcebook for multicultural families / Myra Alperson.
p. cm.
Includes bibliographical references.
ISBN 0-374-52611-7 (alk. paper)
1. Intercountry adoption. 2. Interracial adoption. 3. Ethnicity in children. 4. Family. 5. Multiculturalism. I. Title.

HV875.5 .A434 2001
362.7'34'0973—dc21

00-060971

Designed by Lisa Stokes

To my darling daughter, Sadie

contents

foreword

In the 1950s when children from Korea were adopted by families in the United States and Europe, assimilating adoptees was given priority over providing them connection to their birth culture and identity. "Fitting in" and "belonging" were considered the measures of success. That was nearly five decades ago, and we have grown up. We did assimilate. In communities throughout the United States we became a part of the culture and identity of our adopted families and communities. Often isolated, the first generation of international adoptees grew up not knowing another person "who looked like me." We identified with the lives we were living, not with the lives we were born into.

I grew up in a small rural community in Oregon where I was the only Asian. I did not meet another Korean adoptee until I was seventeen years old. I have never forgotten what an incredibly important moment that was for both of us. To finally see someone who looked like me, who knew without words what it was like to live in my skin. To look Korean but not feel Korean.

Like other adoptive families during those early years of

intercultural adoption, my parents did not have examples of how to parent a child of another race and culture. Their true emotional relationship to me as their daughter was not affected by those differences. But the reality is that intercultural families *look* different, and many people hold the belief that the family *relationships* are different, that they are not as "real." Parents adopting a child of another race and culture must learn early on to assume the role of advocating for the "realness" of their family since they will be called upon to validate it, often to people they have never met before.

What adoptive families must learn is to separate the feelings and connection of family from the differences of culture and identity that exist between parents and children—not to fear the differences, but to embrace them. To be honest about them and confront them boldly. To prepare to meet the challenges that can sometimes be truly painful as well as joyful.

Parents will not always have the answers or be able to prevent or protect their children from the hurts and slights of a world that does not always acknowledge differences and diversity as a blessing. *Dim Sum, Bagels, and Grits* helps families develop a clearer understanding of their membership in this unique community of families. Written with insight and candor from the perspective of professionals as well as those who have lived the experience, this book is a thoughtful and practical resource to guide, support, and encourage parents as they anticipate and live the reality of intercultural families. It should be on the shelf of anyone considering intercultural adoption so that later it may be shared with the extended family and friends, or adoption practitioners working with intercultural families.

Individuals of any race or culture do not outgrow the longing to be connected—to have a sense of belonging, to be with others who are "just like me," and to know they are a part of a broader community. As parents of intercultural adoptees encourage their children to explore and come to peace with who they are, they and their children will broaden the possibilities for all of us in the global community.

Susan Soon-Keum Cox, Eugene, Oregon

introduction

Families Don't Look the Way They Used To

One day when my daughter, Sadie, was just three she briefly lost sight of me at a playground and started crying for Mommy. A father in the playground took her hand to try to help out. As I walked toward her shouting her name, he was looking in another direction. Then he realized, with a jolt, that the white woman yelling "Sadie!"—me—was her mother. But it wasn't automatic. Sadie is Chinese. He walked her over to me.

As more families adopt across racial, ethnic, and cultural boundaries, stories like mine are increasingly common. Since the late 1990s, more than sixteen thousand children have been adopted from other countries each year, usually from backgrounds different from the parents'. Within the United States, too, thousands of children who need homes find them each year with parents of a different race or ethnicity. Over the last four decades, several hundred thousand children have been adopted cross-culturally.

Along with a rise in ethnic and racial intermarriage as well as an increase in single parenting and "older" parenting, adoption is transforming the American family. Even the Supreme Court recently acknowledged that parenting in the United States isn't what it used to be. As Justice Sandra Day O'Connor remarked in a June 2000 ruling related to parental rights, "The demographic changes of the past century make it difficult to speak of an average American family."

For multicultural adoptive families, her statement has special resonance. In choosing to cross cultures to form our families, we have chosen to change many of the former "givens" of what family life and home life are supposed to be. Our children, coming from a different background, are being raised not just by new parents, but in a new culture. What responsibility do we have to "remind" them of what came before—especially if they joined us as infants and their actual memory and experience of their birth family and culture are limited?

Based on Sadie's experience described above, and on what many of our children may grapple with as they grow up knowing that another set of parents gave them life, I think we have a substantial responsibility to honor our children's heritage. And one way to do it is to develop a positive vision of ourselves as a multicultural family living in a multicultural home. That's why I wrote *Dim Sum, Bagels, and Grits*, the first sourcebook for multicultural families formed through adoption.

I believe I speak for many adoptive parents when I express a deep sense of obligation to ensure that my daughter knows about the cultural heritage she was born into as well as the one she is growing up with—and that she feels great about both! As children grow older, they are bound to have encounters similar to the one Sadie had in the playground, in which other people make assumptions about who they are. But these encounters will be more complex, and possibly hurtful, and we won't always be there to fend for our kids. If we can nurture children who are strong and self-confident about who they are—and in Sadie's case, this means Chinese, American, Jewish, my daughter, herself—then we will have done our job.

A Multicultural "Revolution"

The timing for *Dim Sum, Bagels, and Grits* could not be better. Not only is multicultural adoption skyrocketing, but so is its public profile. Media mogul Steven Spielberg and his wife, actress Kate Capshaw; novelist Tama Janowitz; Senator John McCain; and football champ Dan Marino have gone public about adopting children from ethnic and racial backgrounds different from their own, not just because they did it, but also to promote this wonderful way to "grow" a family.

Olympic star Dan O'Brien, who is biracial, grew up in a family with several siblings who were adopted from a range of backgrounds, and he discusses the impact his family situation had on his development. Mainstream magazines report on folks like him—potential role models for our children. Oprah Winfrey and Rosie O'Donnell spotlight adoption on their shows. (Rosie's Web site includes adoption information.) Ads by Compaq Computer, Merrill Lynch, and Procter & Gamble feature families like ours. In its attempt to present itself as a socially responsible company, Wendy's, the fast-food chain, promotes adoption. Wendy's CEO Dave Thomas makes no secret of the fact that he's proud that he was adopted.

Recent waves of immigration have complemented our own journeys into multiculturalism, bringing new flavors, sounds, and looks to the American mainstream. Fashions drawing on African, Asian, and Latino influences are sold in shopping malls. Schools nationwide celebrate "International Day" to acknowledge the diversity of their student body, while the media bring foreign worlds into our homes.

Multicultural toys are being made, and children of many colors are showing up in clothing ads and books—and not just when the story line is ethnic. Publishers and toymakers aren't creating these products to be nice. Multicultural families are an increasing fact of life—and a growing market.

What This Book Does

Dim Sum, Bagels, and Grits has two principal goals. First, it seeks to understand what it means to be multicultural through our own and our children's experiences. Through interviews conducted around the United States with large and small families, headed by single parents and couples, I've gathered a range of strategies for how to create balance in adoptive families, no matter where the parents live or what extenuating circumstances might affect our ability to provide the best possible cultural ambiance for our children. I've talked to a number of adoptees to glean their insights on how they experienced being adopted and how they observe cross-cultural adoption today. I've also interviewed several experts on multicultural adoption to explore some of the key issues and trends our families face. (Some of these people are also adoptive parents.)

Second, the book aims to provide a compendium of resources that can help us create and strengthen multicultural homes.

I start with the basics—looking first at a history of cross-cultural adoption and what it means to become a multicultural family. I then examine the process of making an adoption happen. Next I explore such nuts and bolts as the best places to live, how to find appropriate childcare or schools, deciding how religious preferences will be preserved within the family (if this is relevant for you), bringing our children's original culture and language into our home, and finding mentors for our children. I examine special concerns of parents adopting older children, such as whether to keep the children's birth names and whether children should retain their birth language in their new country, as well as how to help children make the adjustment to a new culture and family.

I examine the question of family trees. At different junctures in their lives, our children are bound to confront questions of where they "belong" in their family structure. One of the more riveting anecdotes I have come across describes the painful experience of an adult adoptee discovering that a beloved aunt never really quite considered her part of the family. Let's look into how to create an alternative to the family tree that's as flexible and inclusive as our own families.

Because many of us will, regrettably, encounter some form of prejudice expressed toward our children and our family unit (and anti-adoption attitudes in general), I've devoted a chapter to exploring the many forms of prejudice, and I've provided first-person accounts of how other families have responded. At times, what we interpret as prejudice may be ignorance—but we must still find a way to respond to it for our children's sake. If we can learn to "gently educate," we will have done others a great service!

As our children grow older, new identity issues become a natural part of the growing process, and we may be caught off guard if we're not ready, watching, and listening. When our children look different from us (and from many of their friends), they may confront new layers of anxiety and questions of greater complexity in their teen years. (Some children will experience a sense of "apartness" more acutely than others. Every child is different, and there is no "uniform" response to growing pains.)

A comprehensive Resources section lists an array of publications and goods and services for our families: catalogs, magazines, and newsletters; books for adults and children; toys, gifts, cards, and related items; food resources; organizations; culture camps; and homeland tours.

Since food often plays an important role in a multicultural household, I had envisioned a chapter of recipes and went to the effort of soliciting recipes from parents, but I scrapped the idea after I queried an e-mail discussion group of adoptive parents and received a number of responses similar to this one: "Microwave macaroni and cheese: Stick it in the oven, cook for three minutes, serve." Instead, I include a section on ethnic food resources in Chapter 8. You'll also find recipes at a number of Web sites mentioned in Chapters 7 and 8, and several children's books in Chapter 7 have food as a theme and include recipes.

Adoptees Take the Lead

In the course of my research, I've had opportunities to talk with some of the newer leaders in the multicultural adoption community. These people are adoptees themselves, now grownup and asserting themselves in the world. They are challenging us—and society in general—to *listen*, to accept them for who they are, to understand that last names don't necessarily dictate our ethnic origins, to take their issues seriously, and to be responsible in understanding their complex needs and decisions.

Older adoptees are forming organizations; holding meetings; producing magazines, videos, and books; and exploring the legacy of intercultural adoption as they enter adulthood. Best of all, they are sharing their observations and experiences with us. And many speak with pride of belonging to a multicultural family. I cannot tell you how reassuring it was to read the charter of the organization of Korean adoptees called Also-Known-As, which affirms the positive impact of cross-cultural adoption.

Every child is different. Some may be easygoing about their adoption story. Others may become obsessed about knowing what happened to them, why, how to make sense of it, and how to retrace their roots. We parents have to be prepared, flexible, and open-minded so that we can respond.

part i

we are family

one

Who We Are

The Facts

I believe that when you become a multiethnic family, you need to change almost as much as the child who joins you. That doesn't mean that you have to cook only Korean food or speak Korean, but you have to be very open to it, and it has to become part of you in some way. If you don't feel that you can somehow identify with this ethnic group, then transcultural adoption is probably not for you!

—Seattle mother of four children, two born in Korea, two biological

A Critical Mass

In September 1999 the first international convocation of Korean adoptees—organized by the adoptees themselves—took place in Washington, D.C. Some four hundred adoptees from the United States and Europe took part. This event was a milestone. It represented the first time that adoptees, most in their twenties and thirties, had taken ownership in such a visible and significant way of the dialogue and debate on what it means to be adopted across cultures.

Although the events were closed to non-adoptees, I followed the discussions closely, as reports came in on adoption listservs. I also met with some of the organizers. The more I talked with them, the more it became clear that I had a lot to learn, and that the process would be lifelong. Some of the adoptees had taken Korean names; others had kept their American surnames and flaunted them with pride. Some had made a relentless search in Korea to try to find their birth parents; for others this journey was not a priority. And, of course, some adoptees chose to stay home.

Through a Web site related to this gathering, I gained access to a forum that enabled me to experience vicariously the give-and-take between adoptees and parents. Would this be Sadie and me in fifteen years? In each case I was struck by the range of responses, many fraught with emotion. Some grown adoptees reported harboring an abiding hurt over being separated from their birth family. Others were filled with exhilaration at being able to share their life experiences. It was like a coming out party for many of them. The adoption experience, clearly, is hardly monolithic, on the part of either the parents or the adoptees. Coming to terms with being adopted, and being an adoptive parent, can be an ongoing struggle. Parents are particularly tested when children approach young adulthood; this phase of any child's life can be particularly trying.

An underlying theme of the gathering of the Korean adoptees was that intercultural adoption can be an empowering and positive process. The vision statement of one of the organizing groups praises intercultural adoption because of the way in which it enables families to "cross borders of race, ethnicity and blood."

As part of a process of preparing to parent my own child from a different background (and to collect materials for this book), over time, I have also listened to young adults born in Latin America as well as black and biracial young adults adopted by white and interracial families within the United States discuss their experiences and dilemmas growing up. In talking to parents whose experiences crossing cultures had preceded mine by many years, I came to realize two critical points. One was that I was hardly alone in my concerns. The second was that it was essential to keep my learning in context—and never to stop listening. Families that adopted from the 1950s through the 1970s, when much less information was available, perhaps had more issues to struggle with and far fewer resources to turn to, including other families who were facing the same challenges. There just weren't as many—and the sharing that comes naturally to many families these days wasn't so automatic then.

Thirty or forty years ago there was little knowledge of what it meant to be cross-cultural, either. The idea was to be *American* and to leave as much of the past behind as possible. As a consequence, many parents later found themselves doing a quick course in "catch-up" as their children grew older. Pat Palmer, an Iowa mother who has adopted seven children in all, five from Korea who are now in their thirties and two younger children from Vietnam (she also has two birth children), reports:

> When my children were young, I was eager to find out anything I could about the experiences of those parents who had adopted Korean children ahead of me, but no one was talking. Parenting Korean children was still at the "experimental stage," and I guess most of those involved didn't want to admit to their detractors, who said intercountry adoption wouldn't

work, that everything wasn't perfect, and so all problems were kept quiet. There were rumors, but not many were talking. And the Korean adoptees themselves hadn't grown up, so they too weren't discussing their experiences.

Over the course of the 1960s and 1970s, key adoption alliances were formed, the adoption literature expanded (the magazine *Ours*, later renamed *Adoptive Families*, made its debut in the 1970s), and the number of adoption agencies handling interracial and international adoptions began to multiply. National adoption organizations gained in stature and influence. The first culture camps were organized.

As families' experiences with cross-cultural adoption increased, more information became available. Several studies have shown that children adopted interracially generally grow up with their self-esteem and identity intact—provided that their adoptive parents understand the implications of adopting across racial and cultural boundaries and respond accordingly.

Some negative media images of cross-cultural adoption also emerged—particularly in 1972, when the National Association of Black Social Workers (NABSW) pronounced its opposition to interracial adoption. At a conference that year of the North American Council on Adoptable Children in St. Louis, the president of NABSW gave the keynote speech to an audience that included many white parents who had adopted black children. He accused the parents of committing "cultural genocide" and said that these children could not form a sense of black pride or black identity in such families. Despite claims by advocates of interracial adoption that there were not enough families for black children needing homes,

NABSW maintained that the opposite was true, but that bureaucratic restrictions were preventing placements from taking place. Among other reactions to the NABSW's controversial stance was the departure of some of its members and the passage of a resolution by the National Association for the Advancement of Colored People (NAACP) supporting interracial adoption. Nonetheless, as a result of NABSW's public statement, interracial adoption placements declined dramatically through the rest of the 1970s and into the early 1980s.

Meanwhile, parents did their best. Kirstin Nelson, the biracial daughter (now a thirty-two-year-old law school graduate) of a Nebraska couple who adopted other biracial children, reports:

> My favorite childhood books were from the *Little House* series (it was my favorite TV show, too), and I also loved *Nancy Drew*. I distinctly remember my parents trying to guide me toward books on Harriet Tubman and other stories with black characters and themes. I did read many of those books, but the *Little House* books remained my favorites. I really don't think it made any difference in the long run whether I read or played "Little House" or "Underground Railroad"—although I did both over the years.
>
> I think the best thing to do is provide as many options as possible but let your kids make their own choices and decisions about what they are interested in. There is a fine line between guidance and over-parenting.

By the 1990s, the cumulative numbers of interracial and international adoptions, along with ease of access to adoption information via the Internet, transformed the adoption process. With little more than a keyboard and a modem (and a credit card), we could get most of the information we needed to learn how to adopt, where to adopt, how to find families like ours, and how to hook up with support networks.

These days, the questions I raised about my own ability to raise a child born in another culture and of another ethnicity are being echoed more widely as many more families are being created or are expanding through multicultural adoption. Recommendations on how to move forward are far easier to come by. Discussion groups on the Internet enable parents with common adoption interests, wherever they live, to share information. And the e-commerce revolution makes it possible to obtain difficult-to-find books, clothing, food, music, and other resources and to develop a multicultural environment for our families, whether we live in a rural area or a large city.

Yet merely acquiring multicultural materials and taking part in cultural activities will not address our children's emotional and psychological needs as cross-cultural adoptees, nor will these approaches to parenting our children make up for the fact that they have lost something most of us take for granted: their birth culture. As parents we need to recognize that being a multicultural family is not something to celebrate only on special occasions; it is a fact of our daily lives. Being vigilant of the needs of children whom Pat Palmer aptly describes as "double minorities," that is, adoptees who do not share their parents' ethnic background, must be a key element in our overall approach to parenting.

How Cross-Cultural Adoptions Began

To put this discussion into context, I think it helps to understand how and why cross-cultural adoptions came about in the first place, and what the current patterns and trends appear to be.

INTERCOUNTRY ADOPTIONS

Cross-cultural adoption from outside the United States began in a significant way in the late 1940s, when homes were sought for European children orphaned during World War II and following the Greek Civil War. Occasionally we read accounts of these orphans—now grownup and connecting with their roots, or perhaps seeking lost relatives—but the adoptees tend to be scattered.

Cross-racial adoptions of Korean children orphaned in the Korean War began in the 1950s. Many of these children were ethnically mixed—their mothers were Korean and their fathers were of the race or ethnicity of the various military forces involved in the conflict. Because Korean society rejected children born out of wedlock—and ostracized their mothers—most of these mixed-race children were rejected by their biological families and placed in institutions. Koreans were not prepared to raise mixed-race children.

Neither, to some extent, were people in the United States. These early adoptions represented, in the words of Madelyn Freundlich, former executive director of the Evan B. Donaldson Adoption Institute in New York City, a type of "crazy social experiment." Children from a specific Asian culture were placed with families in the United States who generally knew little or nothing about that culture. In those days it was rare for families to travel to Korea to adopt; in almost all cases the children were escorted by adoption professionals on the long plane ride to the United States (certainly longer in those days than it is now!), and their first encounter with their new family was in an airport.

Imagine this experience reported by Pat Palmer when her family attended its first potluck supper with other adoptive families in the early 1970s:

> There we were with our four young children—five, three, three, and one, two by birth and two by adoption—with families who had adopted in the early to mid-sixties and their school-age children. A minister and his wife led the program afterward and introduced a song they had written for the occasion, which we all sang. It was a sad little dirge entitled "Who Needs Me?" about Korean orphans and their rescuers/adoptive parents. I looked around the room at the school-age Korean children and wondered what they were thinking. I was glad my children, all four of them, were too young to understand.

The international adoption of Korean children (mainly in the United States but also in some European countries, and overwhelmingly by white couples) continued over the next four decades for a number of reasons. First, as Korean adoptions became more widely known and perceived as "successful," infertile couples seeking healthy newborns sought to adopt from Korea. Second, Korea itself did not have a tradition of adoption, and the state infrastructure for caring for orphaned and abandoned children was overburdened. Seeing that families in the United States and Europe were willing to adopt children whose own families could not care for them, Korea established formal agreements with overseas agencies to make the process more efficient. From the mid-1950s to 2000, close to 100,000 children were adopted by families in the United States. In all, some 141,000 Korean children were adopted worldwide during that period.

In the intervening decades, international adoption grew in waves, with some countries dominating placements at different times. During the early 1990s the numbers stayed steady at about 7,000 to 9,000 per year. But during the second half of the decade they gradually veered upward. More than 16,000 "orphan visas" were issued in 1999 by the U.S. State Department, owing to a number of factors:

- Adoption itself was becoming a more popular way to form or expand a family.
- More older couples and single people were adopting (thanks, in large part, to sponsor countries formulating policies that welcome these people to apply).
- More employers were adding adoption support to their benefits packages.
- More countries that lacked the capacity to care for abandoned children adequately were creating programs to make adoption possible.
- The breakup of the Soviet Union and more outreach to the West increased adoption opportunities in some of the newly formed countries of what had been the Eastern bloc.

- Increased contact with China also led to increased opportunities for Western families to adopt Chinese children, mostly girls.
- The Internet streamlined the adoption process. In addition to private agencies going on-line, the State Department published adoption guidelines and offered essential forms on-line that families needed to file with the Immigration and Naturalization Service to get the process going.
- In 2000, new legislation granted automatic United States citizenship to internationally adopted children.
- More information on cross-cultural adoption became generally available, both in print and via electronic media.
- Finally, cross-cultural adoption itself became more "socially acceptable" in line with overall social trends.

THE NUMBERS ON INTERNATIONAL ADOPTION

We have solid data on international cross-cultural adoptions because the Immigration and Naturalization Service (INS) tracks the numbers of immigrant visas issued to adopted children.

To give you an idea of how adoption patterns change, here's a sampling of the number of international adoptions in the United States in 1989, 1994, and 1999, based on the number of visas issued to children who were adopted by U.S. citizens.

	1989		1994		1999	
	Country	Visas Issued	Country	Visas Issued	Country	Visas Issued
1	S. Korea	3,544	S. Korea	1,795	Russia	4,348
2	Colombia	736	Russia	1,530	China	4,101
3	India	648	China	787	S. Korea	2,008
4	Philippines	465	Paraguay	483	Guatemala	1,002
5	Chile	253	Guatemala	436	Romania	895
6	Paraguay	252	India	412	Vietnam	709
7	Peru	222	Colombia	314	India	499
8	Guatemala	202	Philippines	314	Ukraine	321
9	China	201	Vietnam	220	Cambodia	249
10	Honduras	181	Romania	199	Colombia	231
11	Brazil	175	Ukraine	164	Bulgaria	221
12	Romania	138	Brazil	149	Philippines	195
13	Thailand	109	Bulgaria	97	Mexico	137
14	Cuba	95	Lithuania	95	Kazakhstan	113
15	El Salvador	94	Poland	94	Ethiopia	103
16	Mexico	91	Mexico	85	Poland	97
17	Haiti	80	Chile	79	Haiti	96
18	Costa Rica	78	Honduras	77	Thailand	77
19	Taiwan	75	Haiti	61	Brazil	66
20	Japan	74	Ethiopia	54	Lithuania	63
21	Poland	74	Japan	49	Moldova	63
	Total for top 21 countries: 7,787		Total for top 21 countries: 7,494		Total for top 21 countries: 15,594	
	Visas worldwide: 8,102		Visas worldwide: 8,333		Visas worldwide: 16,396	

Source: United States State Department, Immigration and Naturalization Service

Some adoption patterns have changed dramatically. China and Russia, which barely registered on the adoption radar screen in 1989, each processed more than four thousand adoptions in 1999.

Although data on the age and marital status of adoptive parents have not been formally collected, many agencies report that the types of households now adopting children are changing and more nontraditional families are adopting children. A contributing factor, as has already been noted, is the growing number of employers, from universities to corporations and federal agencies, that are extending parental leave benefits to families who are adopting. (*Working Woman* magazine lists adoption benefits as one of its criteria for selecting the "100 Best Companies for Women.")

Just ten years ago, I would have had far fewer options, as a single woman over forty, to adopt. China didn't have a formal program yet, and the few countries that did were not welcoming applicants like me. Adoption e-mail discussion groups now include subgroups of "older" parents, and several new books focus on guiding single individuals through the adoption labyrinth, including tips on money management, estate preparation, childcare, and other concerns. We've come a long way, in a relatively short time, from the days when women in my situation had to search long and hard, sometimes for years, to find an adoption agency that would help us fulfill our quest to become parents. In her book *Family Bonds*, Elizabeth Bartholet describes her own harrowing quest to adopt in Latin America in the mid-1980s as an older single woman. Although the book came out in 1993—not so long ago—the adoption process and the attitudes toward older, single women adopting have changed dramatically since then.

DOMESTIC DATA ARE HARDER TO MEASURE

The number of children adopted domestically by families of a different background than their own is far harder to measure. Historically, interracial adoption within the United States only began to grow in significant numbers in the 1960s. The introduction of the birth control pill meant that fewer babies—especially white babies—would be placed for adoption. Therefore many white couples turned to interracial domestic adoption to form their families. As many as twenty thousand such placements had occurred by the time the NABSW issued its statement against interracial adoption in 1972.

Interracial placements stalled for several years until federal and state legislation—and public pressure—loosened restrictions on cross-racial adoptions. Many more black children than white children were waiting for permanent homes. (Constance Pohl and Kathy Harris, authors of *Transracial Adoption*, note that despite reforms, the numbers of minority children awaiting placement rose in the 1990s. Bureaucratic red tape seemed to be largely to blame, as well as a preference by adoptive parents for younger, emotionally healthy children. In some cases, parents-to-be opt for foreign adoption because the process often moves more quickly than it does in domestic adoption, and some parents feel they are more likely to be matched with healthier and younger children. Furthermore, fewer babies are being placed for adoption within the United States, prompting more parents to look abroad.)

The NABSW position against interracial adoption had an important positive outcome: it stressed the need for families who *did* undertake cross-racial adoption to understand their responsibilities to maintain their children's racial identity. That legacy can be seen even to this day in adoption training, whether prospective parents seek to adopt across cultures from within the United States or from another country.

The National Adoption Information Clearinghouse (NAIC), an offshoot of the U.S. Department of Health and Human Services, maintains a database of adoptions in the United States. But getting consistent figures is difficult, the NAIC reports. There has been no organized national data collection on adoption since 1975. The quality of reporting that does exist varies widely by state, and current figures are often based on educated guesses. For the purposes of this book, after analyzing a range of NAIC data, including those on foster care placements, we can make a broad estimate that there are, nowadays, from 10,000 to 25,000 domestic interracial adoptions per year.

PUBLIC PERCEPTIONS OF ADOPTION

An important milestone in adoption awareness was marked in 1997 with the release of a benchmark survey by the Evan B. Donaldson Adoption Institute in New York City. The survey of 1,554 adults reviewed public perceptions and contact with adoption. The results give a clear picture of how much progress multicultural families have made in gaining recognition for themselves since the 1950s (recognition gained through positive *and* negative media exposure). Particularly revealing were the following findings:

- Six in ten Americans have had personal experience with adoption, meaning that they reported that they themselves, a family member, or a close friend was adopted, had adopted a child, or had placed a child for adoption. Those who have had firsthand experience are more supportive of adoption than those who haven't.

- Although most Americans (90 percent) view adoption very favorably or somewhat favorably, many Americans (64 percent) have never considered adopting a child, and about half (49 percent) believe that adoption is not quite as good as raising one's own biological child.

- Women embrace adoption more fully than men do. Thirty-six percent of women express unqualified support compared with 27 percent of men.

- Three times as many whites (35 percent) as blacks (11 percent) are full supporters of adoption.

- Nearly half of Americans (45 percent) say that family members and friends are their main source of information about adoption, whereas 30 percent get their information from news sources and 16 percent from magazines.

- Half of those surveyed (52 percent) believe children adopted from other countries are more likely than children adopted in this country to have emotional problems, and nearly the same proportion (48 percent) say children from abroad are less likely to be physically healthy. On the other hand, most Americans do not believe that children adopted internationally are any more likely to have trouble in school than children adopted from within this country.

DIFFERENT PERCEPTIONS OF ADOPTION WITHIN ADOPTIVE FAMILIES

Although one of the great joys of being a multicultural family is that we can enjoy diversity within our own family unit, one of the hassles can be that our families stand out as "obviously" different in the larger community, so we may be called upon to "explain" ourselves. One reason that some white couples (and some singles) seek to adopt white children is to form the type of family the adoptive parents "might have had" if they had given birth. Another motivation may be to avoid the hassles of having to explain differences, particularly if the family lives in a community that may seem less than accepting.

But an important aspect of "who we are" is facing the fact of adoption honestly, particularly by families whose adopted child resembles her parents enough that it seems unnecessary to highlight the different cultural background and lack of blood ties. White parents who adopt white children, even when their ethnic roots are not the same, may feel that emphasizing differences will not promote a cohesive family unit.

A friend of mine who is the adoptive father of two children from Romania admitted that he felt uncomfortable when the magazine then known as *Ours* was renamed *Adop-*

tive Families in 1994. To him, *Ours* sounded better because the title did not stigmatize the adoptive family as being other, and therefore different from "conventional" families. Both he and his wife share their children's East European ancestry (but not their birth religion). You wouldn't know from meeting the parents and their two kids that the family came together through adoption.

These parents, nevertheless, acknowledge that the adoption story must be told, and that their children's heritage is part of it. So they have always talked openly about the circumstances surrounding the adoption, and the family's two adoption trips to Romania. (They have met the birth mother of their children, who are half-siblings.) They have Romanian artifacts in their home.

But what if these children were born in, say, Eastern Europe, and the parents' ethnic origin was, say, Irish or Italian? What if the parents themselves represented two different religions, and the child's roots were different from both parents'? Should we make room for all the heritages in such a family?

Even if our adopted children's background is similar to ours, don't we owe it to our children to preserve some of their birth heritage? Is it fair—whether they came to us as infants or as somewhat older children—to erase a portion of their unique roots—and their very own story? If we do cut out this aspect of their lives, how will we prepare them for the questions that may come later?

You might say, as some parents do, that adopted children should not have to face an additional identity trauma by being bombarded with reminders of where they came from. When I told the social worker who wrote my home study that I was thinking of hiring a Chinese baby-sitter for Sadie since I wanted to promote the use of Chinese language and customs in our home, she gently scolded me: "She's going to be your daughter raised in an American household. You can give her as much Chinese culture as you want, but don't confuse her!" She feared that my daughter might identify more closely with such a sitter than with me. (I'm sure the response would have been different if I had been a Chinese-American. And I know quite a few adoptive parents who disagree with this stance and have hired Chinese nannies.)

On the other hand, without creating identity confusion, we can expose our children to their birth culture—and share it—as one aspect of our family life, just as we observe birthdays and holidays. It's part of who we are.

Who We Are—in the Twenty-first Century

In ways that I sometimes think elude many parents—and perhaps critics of multiculturalism—our children are growing up in a world that *is* increasingly multicultural, and they're experiencing the phenomenon in a far different way than we are, especially if we grew up in the 1950s and 1960s. The pervasiveness of multiculturalism in our daily lives, in any family's daily life, makes parenting our kind of family easier and potentially much more fulfilling. For the same reason, I worry a bit less about some of the stigmas traditionally attached to adoption; there's just too much adoption for people to view it pejoratively the way they once did.

We increasingly find that our children's values and activities are part of a global values system (catalyzed, for better or worse, by the growing impact of "global brands," such as McDonald's, Levi's, and Sony, as well as by the media).

Teenagers the world over dress more and more alike (including dyeing their hair different colors and piercing odd parts of their body), listen to the same music (rap is a global phenomenon), play the same computer games, and identify with the same teen idols. They cheer worldwide for such "crossover" phenomena as Ricky Martin and Jackie Chan. And, of course, they take the Internet for granted.

Okay, so the world is changing. But who *are* we *now*? How truly significant is the "multicultural" family in the United States? In particular, where does the multicultural family stand in the big picture, which includes multicultural, multiracial families formed through marriage?

THE GROWING INFLUENCE OF MULTICULTURALISM

There are many anecdotal examples to demonstrate the growing influence of multiculturalism on American families, regardless of whether the families were formed through adoption or through birth. As a parent, I encounter these phenomena often. They include the following:

- There is a proliferation of international activities in our children's schools, starting as early as nursery school. "International Days" are now often part of the curricula. More enlightened schools promote a range of holidays, so that Christmas and Chanukah are just two of the several holiday traditions children are exposed to. (My daughter's nursery school even celebrates Tet, a Southeast Asian holiday.) Many children also learn about Diwali, the Hindu Festival of Lights; Ramadan, the Muslim period of fasting; Kwanzaa, the African-

American winter celebration that draws on African and African-American ideas and traditions to celebrate history, culture, and community; and the lunar new year observed in much of the Far East.

- In growing numbers of children's books, children of various racial and ethnic backgrounds are depicted, without necessarily being part of the story. Authors such as Helen Oxenbury and Vera Williams have developed a following of readers who take for granted the multihued families that populate their stories.
- The theme of diversity is key to the story in a growing number of children's books. Such books would not be published if there were no market for them. An excellent example is Anti-Bias Books for Kids, published by Redleaf Press. Each book includes characters of different ethnic backgrounds, and one of them usually has a physical disability, but is mainstreamed with friends. Many publishers now have divisions that specialize in multicultural themes. The Hyperion imprint "Follow the Sun" emphasizes books on African-American subjects. (See Chapter 7, Publications.)
- Toys are more deliberately multicultural today. Companies such as Crayola and Mattel (the maker of Barbie) have created "multicultural" product lines. Some smaller companies focus exclusively on offering culturally diverse products.
- There is a growing industry of catalogs and on-line resources for multicultural books and toys, targeting par-

ents who have adopted cross-culturally (and who tend to be older and more affluent than most families in general). Quite a few owners of such companies are adoptive parents themselves, who have started a cottage industry of home-based businesses that produce goods and services for this market.

- Mainstream children's television programming places a greater emphasis on multiculturalism, with pioneering shows such as *Sesame Street* leading the way.

We see increased examples of multiculturalism in our adult lives, too.

- Ethnic food—well beyond Chinese and Italian—is more widely available at restaurants and in cookbooks; these days ethnic fast food can be found in the freezer sections of many supermarkets.
- "World music" has gained popularity, helped along by performers such as Paul Simon and David Byrne, who have cultivated partnerships with musicians on every continent. (Who would have imagined just a few years ago seeing the South African ensemble Ladysmith Black Mambazo—which performs in the Zulu language—singing backup for a commercial for LifeSavers candy?)
- There is more interest in dance styles from Latin America and elsewhere in the world.
- Publications celebrate ethnic consciousness, often through fashion.

- The media is putting more emphasis on arts and literature created by foreign-born artists and writers who, in their work, introduce us to their cultures.

- Ethnic fashion has reached the mainstream. How many moms wore Indian "peasant" skirts when they were younger? Bold African and Latin American colors and patterns are integrated into children's and adult clothing. Remember Mao and Nehru jackets? These days, African *kente* patterns, Indonesian batiks, and Guatemalan weavings have influenced all sorts of clothing and accessories—and not only for college students.

- Especially in cities, there is a general awareness of the increasingly multicultural nature of our society, spurred by increased emigration from East and West Africa, regions of south and Southeast Asia and Eastern Europe, as well as from all over Latin America.

As one parent writes:

> My wife is Chinese and I am Caucasian, and we have been married eighteen years. In the early years we would get a lot of looks and double takes. As the years passed, Eurasian families and Eurasian children in our community became much more common. We don't warrant a second look today.

Many schools now include "dual-language" programs not just for children for whom English is their second (or third) language, but as a learning opportunity for children who speak English as their first language. The goal here, as I understand it, is both to strengthen the mastery of English for second-language learners and to create a balance and appreciation among students for the language and culture of an ethnic group that may have a significant presence in the community.

For those students whose primary experience of learning English takes place outside the home, the dual-language approach to learning also removes the stigma of being "different." And some studies are now showing that children learning in two languages do at least as well as their counterparts learning in monolingual settings.

YOUNG ADOPTED ADULTS LEAD THE WAY

For me, a more significant index of the acceptance gained by multicultural families is the growing number of resources available and of activities that are organized for them, often by adults who were adopted cross-culturally. Nationally known adoption professionals and advocates such as Deborah Johnson and Susan Soon-Keum Cox speak widely on cross-cultural issues. Johnson also guides homeland tours to Korea and other countries. These advocates, and the activities they have created, make the work of parenting a multicultural family easier and richer.

I have been deeply influenced by my own conversations with adult adoptees. They are the leaders that parents should look to with questions about addressing our children's identity issues.

The Korean adoption community—mainly through the efforts of the organization Also-Known-As—has spearheaded an amazing array of activities, including discussion forums, a magazine called *TransCultured*, an outstanding Web site, cultural events, cooking and language classes, homeland visits, and mentoring programs for younger adopted kids. Launched just in 1997, Also-Known-As is an excellent guidepost for those of us who have adopted younger children across cultural lines.

Of course, Also-Known-As became viable when there was a large enough group of grownup Korean adoptees who shared similar experiences about what it meant to be adopted and raised in communities unfamiliar with adoption and by parents of different races or ethnicities. Many of these adoptees were raised at a time when promoting a separate cultural awareness was something that adoptive families simply did not do. The children were considered *American*—and that was that.

As adults, some of these adoptees have embarked on personal journeys to trace their roots, get to know one another, and assert their identities in ways that suit their own needs. Pat Palmer notes that her adopted children went through various identity struggles throughout adolescence, and emerged into very different—and, she says, successful—people in adulthood.

> Our Korean-American daughter, a professional, has primarily white friends. One Vietnamese-American son, who works for a large pharmaceutical company, is engaged to a Vietnamese immigrant woman and has mostly Asian-American friends. Our other Vietnamese-American son, an inner-city high school teacher, associates mostly with Asian-Americans and Latinos. John, our Korean-American son, focuses on Korea, and as I write he's in Seoul for a month during his university's Christmas break.

> John called the three years he lived in Korea (studying for his master's degree) "the most excruciating experience in my life, yet there is no other place I would rather be. I was engulfed into the mainstream of society for the first time in my life, where I was judged by my abilities not by my race. As I continued to build my language skills and cultural awareness I became more Korean every day. Although America is where I live, Korea is now my home." John recently wrote to me, "Being a Korean adoptee puts you in 'Never Never Land' until you make a commitment to either side. You are not white AND you are not Korean."

In a documentary called *Crossing Chasms*, Jennifer Arndt, a Korean-American filmmaker, chronicles the experiences of several Korean adoptees who have chosen to live and work in Korea, some to stay, others to visit for a short time. She traces her own wrenching, and ultimately fruitless, quest to locate her birth family, including an awkward meeting, rife with anticipation, with a family that turned out not to be related to her.

Young mixed-race adults, including those born to parents who married interracially and those who were adopted transracially, have become more vocal. The Public Broadcasting System documentary *An American Love Story*, which aired in 1999, explored the life of an interracial couple and their two biracial daughters, and provoked some very interesting debates.

A number of books have also explored the impact of growing up in a multicultural environment. *Half & Half*, a collection of essays by writers whose backgrounds represent two or more cultures, examines precisely what it means to grow up feeling alienated from "mainstream" culture, but unsure where one belongs. *Black, White, Other,* by Lise Funderburg, who is biracial herself, explores the experience of being biracial from the perspective of several dozen people she interviewed, who ranged in age from their twenties to their sixties. But I've been especially intrigued by the appearance of a new magazine created by and for transracial youth called *Mavin*. *Mavin*'s founding editor, Matt Kelley, was a college freshman at Wesleyan University when he started the magazine. *Mavin* is reaching growing numbers of college campuses where a core group of mixed-raced young adults are coming of age and making their presence and their numbers known. The Fall 1999 issue focused on transracial adoption.

A sophisticated, glossy publication, *Mavin* is full of ads touting new youth fashions. Its models epitomize the so-called "exotic" look that is popular in mainstream magazines. But many of the people depicted are, in fact, the very people *Mavin* is reaching out to: people whose racial background is mixed.

Mavin is far more than a magazine. As the product of youth who grew up with the World Wide Web, it also has an active Web site, which serves as a forum in which mixed-race youth can debate with their counterparts on issues that reflect their particular worldview.

I believe there is a common thread to the rise of groups such as Also-Known-As, the creation of *Mavin*, the proliferation of literature on multicultural families, and the development of so much material related to multiculturalism: a special pride that comes from being part of a new type of family within American society.

As Carrie Kent, who has adopted two African-American children, observes:

> Sometimes I feel that adoptive families are very lucky. As we work to learn about and celebrate each other's similarities and differences, we grow as a family. Instead of simply spending all our time looking backward to one set of ancestors to explain who we are in the present, we have multiple layers to explore. And what we create in the end is, I think, wonderfully unique. It's not better than a genetically related family, but it is equally wonderful and special.

two

How We Got There

■

The Journey to Becoming a Multicultural Family

Our youngest son's adoption is very open, and we were at the hospital when he was born. His birth mom had received a certificate for a free mother-child portrait, and she gave it to me to use (a pretty sad moment thinking about the implications of her gesture). Anyhow, I had a picture taken of the two boys (one was two years and one was two months) and myself and hung it proudly in our home. It was in a spot where I could see it often throughout the day.

It had been up for a few weeks when one day I looked at it and thought, "Wow, we really look different from each other!" It seemed to all of a sudden occur to me that no wonder people kept asking about my family. We look so very different. When I look at my kids, I see my kids, but when I looked at that picture that day I saw a white woman, an Asian kid, and a black baby.

—an adoptive mother of two sons, one from Korea, one African-American

A Packing List

When I think about the cross-cultural adoption experience as I now know it, I think of two themes. One is the journey that brought us to cross-cultural adoption. The other is the often unexpected (and evolving) change that happens when the adoptive family is formed.

Our journey to adopt is often fraught with stops and starts as we move forward, because the decision to adopt is very individual, and sometimes scary. As parents-to-be, we bring our own issues and doubts along with us, and that can be a lot of baggage to carry. Some of us started out hoping to give birth, so we may have had a mental image of a child who looked like us. Others started the journey without a partner or without desiring to give birth. For most of us in the latter situation, we were forming a family with a structure that was far different from that of the family we grew up with. We thus bring a combination of curiosity and wariness to our venture into new territory as adoptive parents.

We also have a "packing list" to consider because, unlike biological parents, we have a lot of choices before us. As we map out the trip, we pack past experiences and preconceptions into our decision-making suitcase. Yet, in order for the adoption to come through, we also have to leave extra space. That's where we put our open mind, so that we will be able to "expect the unexpected." This capacity doesn't come easily for everyone.

After you have chosen to adopt cross-culturally, you face a lot of procedures and still further choices: Where to adopt?

What age child? Should you use an agency or a lawyer? and so on.

Some decisions have little to do with the country or the culture: perhaps you wanted to adopt a child, and a particular country currently has an active program of placement with families like yours. You may be like some parents I interviewed who explored a range of adoption options and figured that whichever one worked out first was the one they were "meant" to pursue. Other prospective parents may have direct ties to a particular country or culture because of a previous living or work experience.

Becoming a "Family of Choice"

However we become part of a multicultural family unit, it is important to acknowledge each step we take that leads to forming a new entity called family. Your family unit is no longer just African-American, just Jewish, just Korean, but a new "hybrid" version.

I often laugh at what happened to my own perception of family when I adopted my daughter. Now I was a mother. And although I was still single, I began referring to my past life as "when I was single."

We're lucky folks: families that combine cultures, says family therapist Lascelles Black, can enjoy rich cultural experiences by celebrating and sharing the various rituals, customs, and philosophies each member represents. Our decision to adopt cross-culturally creates a "family of choice" that takes us beyond traditional family boundaries and definitions—and sometimes, he says, away from oppressive family situations and into healthier ones. In a sense, adopting cross-culturally is a privilege: as parents we have a lot of leeway in choosing the cultures from which to adopt. We may choose to bring Asian, Latin American, East European, African-American, or Ethiopian children into our lives. We have access, through our children, to interesting new cultures. We can broaden our lives in exciting ways.

What is key to making such cultural blending work, says Black, who practices in Mount Vernon, New York, is ensuring that the cultures are balanced. For instance, in a family representing two cultures, the children should not be described as "half this and half that," he says. "To say that means that a part of the culture is cut off, and that's wrong. Each 'half' is actually a 'whole.' " Nor should one of the cultures be denied. Some families with biracial (white and African-American) children tend to identify the children as black because, the standard cliché goes, that is how society sees them, and the children will cope better if they can identify with one group rather than feel like eternal outsiders by trying to straddle two.

John Raible, a biracial man who was adopted by white parents and grew up in an all-white community, wrote in 1990 of his firm belief that "people of color [need] to develop a clear, affirming cultural identity in order to minimize the psychological effects of racism," and to avoid the isolation and despair he experienced growing up, particularly as a teenager. In college he chose to attend a public institution rather than a private one, and there, for the first time, he met and gravitated toward African-Americans from middle-class backgrounds similar to his own. Because his family did not fully understand much of what he was going through in his search for identity, he ultimately had to "go it alone" and work out critical issues for himself. In a speech to adoptive parents, he said:

> I am grateful for what I have been given by being adopted. I received a great start to a life as an independent, self-sufficient black man. Now, living on my own, raising my own black son, no longer buffered by white middle-class supports, I must make my way in a hostile, racist society drawing on all the resources at my disposal. For the most part, those resources are found in the black community and in other communities of color.

Although some biracial adoptees have, indeed, chosen to identify with communities of color, others feel they have been shortchanged by not being given equal access to one part of their heritage. A woman I spoke to reported:

> I have a close friend who is biracial (African-American/Italian-American). She was adopted by an Irish-American family at birth, and was raised with as much African-American culture as her parents could provide—biracial siblings, African-American friends in the home, and so forth. However, she had absolutely no knowledge of what it is to be Italian-American. She felt this was a "missing piece of the puzzle," especially since her birth mom was Italian-American. Had her birth mom not arranged for her to be adopted, she most certainly would have been raised steeped in Italian-American culture.
>
> I don't think it's a coincidence that she chose me for a friend: I'm about her birth mom's age and I'm mostly Italian-American. We've spent a lot of time talking about Italian-American culture—and eating. Food is a major part of

Italian-American identity, and she had never eaten "real" Italian-American cooking before.

My point in sharing this is that it is equally important how we see ourselves, even if the world sees us as something else. My friend missed something by not having both sides of her heritage, and she knew it. She very much has the feeling of "these are my people, too." She has since moved to another area, and I miss the time we spent together. I found that I spent more time thinking about what it means to be Italian-American than I have since childhood and the teenage years (when we think a lot about our identities), since someone was asking me about it who had a personal stake in my answers.

If the family doesn't work conscientiously to balance different family needs and views, efforts to integrate two or more cultures in one home can lead to friction. As in the case of the young African-American/Italian-American woman, there can be a gnawing sense that something is missing. Or one or more family members may not fully accept or understand the cultural mix. An undercurrent of prejudice may rise to the surface. "Multicultural issues often provide the basis for some conflicts in cross-cultural relationships," says Lascelles Black. "But the couples I work with may not acknowledge that this is the case and tend to see their differences only as strengths." So it is important to make sure that the home life is balanced and that there is a degree of acceptance from family members—and also that our children are given the freedom to make responsible choices for themselves as they grow up. Our job, as John Raible mentions, is to provide the framework within which this can happen.

For our purposes, of course, the relationships we're exploring are not specifically between spouses or life partners, but between any one family member and another whose background is different. Sometimes the conflict may be between parents. But other times it may involve the children themselves (particularly if there are biological children as well as adopted children in the family), or the grandparents, or other relatives who are part of the larger family matrix, including in-laws, our children's siblings, our own siblings, and people outside our family who may play critical roles in our lives. (See Chapter 5, Confronting Prejudice . . . and Moving Beyond It.)

We may wish to include our relatives in our adoption journey—or, if some of them (not including immediate family members) are less than enthusiastic, we may decide to distance ourselves from them. This is a tricky and potentially painful situation. But if certain people pose a potential obstacle in your journey, you may have to decide between that relationship and what is really important: forming the family *you* want.

Picturing Your Family

It's important to try to *picture your family*. Try to imagine what you will "look" like and some of the issues you may face. If you have your heart set on a child whose background is close to yours, an interracial, cross-cultural adoption may not be for you.

A good resource for preparing to parent children of another race or ethnicity is *I'm Chocolate, You're Vanilla*, a book that explores strategies for raising biracial children. Author

Marguerite Wright, a clinical psychologist, takes the same stance as Lascelles Black, advising parents not to choose one race as the defining race for their children. Rather, she supports creating a family framework that gives equal weight to all backgrounds represented and encourages children to feel self-confident and strong in the identity they *do* have.

As Wright observes, being biracial *isn't* being black *or* white—it's being both, and feeling good about that. She describes an incident involving a four-year-old biracial girl named Katharine. After a sandbox confrontation with a black boy who calls her "whitey," the girl insists that she's *not* white—she's Katharine. The girl's father, Wright says, wants Katharine to be able to understand that she *is* white, but she says, no, she isn't. What *she* means is that she is black *and* white, not just one of them. (And she doesn't like the idea that white, in the context of sandbox dynamics that particular day, is negative.) It is a tricky concept to master, but she has done it, on her own. This choice is ultimately the child's, and as the child grows up, he or she may choose to identify with one specific group.

Similarly, the experience of growing up Asian in America presents its own set of conflicts. Those of us who have participated in adoption discussions are unhappily familiar with such terms as "oreo" and "banana" to label individuals who are racially African-American or Asian but who are accused of "acting" white. In his collection of essays, *The Accidental Asian*, Eric Liu, a second-generation Chinese-American, examines his upbringing by upwardly mobile parents who chose a typical American suburban lifestyle for their family and promoted a moderate exposure to their Chinese cultural roots.

(Liu recalls his visits to his grandmother in New York City's Chinatown, however, with a wrenching intensity, evoking his sense of having missed out on the essence of Chineseness as he grew up.)

Ultimately, Liu attained a version of his parents' American dream, attending an Ivy League university and landing a job in the Clinton White House while still in his twenties. He also married a white woman (nearly half of Asian-Americans under thirty-five marry non-Asians, he notes). He acknowledges the contradictions in his own life:

> Chinese school was only three hours a week, but it too felt like an endless chore. I was a good student, respectful, but what I recall are only the things that distracted me: someone's notebook left in the desk, a line of loopy cursive on the blackboard, the drone of children reading Chinese in slow unison.
>
> One year Dad was the principal and Mom was one of the teachers. We had a great Chinese New Year party that winter. Somebody bought a boxful of hot McDonald's hamburgers.

Ambivalence is often part of the experience—and it's normal.

On the other hand, there is nothing "ambivalent" when the child you are raising is African-American. There are clear issues of race and culture that you—and, more often, your children—will confront, and if you are *not* African-American yourself, then your adoption choice carries added responsibilities. While some of these apply to all cross-cultural adoptions, others, as described below by Lisa Wittorff, the single mother of three African-American children, are specific to that experience. Lisa says:

Being the parent of a black child means that everyone who sees you knows that you have adopted—or that they wonder if that child belongs to you. It means that many strangers will feel permission to ask you questions and give you advice on how to raise your children. It means that your child will have many experiences you have never had to endure, such as being called "nigger" and being subtly discriminated against in ways you might not even notice, because you've not experienced it. It will mean losing friends who don't understand and who (while they may not have said it this way) are uncomfortable with the color of your child's skin.

Besides all that, the most important thing is not how adopting transracially will affect you, but how it will affect your child. How will your child fit into your life? How much can you change your life to provide for the needs of your child? Will your child be the only black child in school? In the family? In town? How are you going to help her learn to fit into the world of black culture? How are you going to feel when she starts dating one of those black teenage boys you're afraid of? What if he listens to rap music and wears baggy pants? What will you think then?

When my children leave home and venture out on their own, my goal for them is to be able to fit in with other black young adults. I've done a lot to work toward that goal, including moving across the city and changing schools so that my children could live in a diverse neighborhood and attend diverse schools. In my adult life, I've always been interested in black culture and already had some black friends before I came to adopt transracially. I also had worked with many black clients and had a lot of secondhand experience of dealing with prejudice and racism.

Even so, adjusting to parenting black children was a big stretch. Parenting, in and of itself, is much harder than I thought it would be. Parenting black children adds yet another layer onto that difficulty. But I love it, and I wouldn't change it.

Getting Started—My Own Story

There are lots of starting points, and that makes it hard. So where to begin? For me, there were three main things to do: talk, read, and join.

TALK, TALK, TALK

Once I began thinking about adopting, my next step was to share my thoughts with anyone I knew who would listen: my sister, close friends, other relatives (including two adult cousins who had been adopted). At that point I mainly knew that I wanted to be a mother, and my heart was not set on a child who "looked like me."

Early family support was important. No one close to me tried to offer advice on the type of adoption I should pursue. My parents vowed to love my child no matter what. My sister pointed me to a close friend who had recently adopted. I found out about organizations and meetings. At my very first seminar, hosted by a local branch of the National Council on Adoptable Children, I learned about the Adoptive Parents Committee (APC) in New York City and began attending its monthly meetings. The APC is an umbrella organization serving all types of adoptive families and families-to-be. For me, meeting people was more important—at that point—than reading books.

At one of these meetings I met a woman who makes a living writing home studies and consulting on adoption issues. A licensed social worker, she is also the adoptive mother of a now-grown Vietnamese/African-American daughter. I made an appointment to see her. I had a problem: I knew I wanted to adopt, but I had no idea where to start. I felt I would be best equipped to raise a girl, but I wasn't even sure if I wanted a baby or a slightly older child.

The social worker's office was festooned with photos of families she had had a hand in forming through her home studies and advice. We spent three hours reviewing a range of issues: my age (forties), my work situation (full-time job, doing some work at home), family support (emotional, yes, and, in emergencies, financial), marital status (single), friends within and outside the adoption community, and my vision of parenting.

Ultimately, the social worker recommended that I adopt from China. Given my age and that I had waited so long to become a parent, she felt that this was the best route for me. Chinese placements could happen fairly quickly, and I could request a very young child (by now I was convinced that I wanted to adopt a baby, since I'd never had baby experience and wanted it at least once in my life). Moreover, the adoptions were organized in a methodical way with the Chinese government. Yet I was startled. The prospect of adopting a child from Asia had registered nowhere on my personal radar screen. So before I moved forward, I had to step back a bit.

FEARS

Chinese culture felt alien to me. I had no close friends of Chinese background. I knew nothing about the Chinese language. Other than my love for Chinese food and the few Chinese movies I'd seen that had gained a lot of acclaim at the time, my appreciation of Chinese culture was limited.

I felt very shy among Chinese people. If I went shopping in Chinatown, I felt as if I was in a foreign country. To adopt a child from China I would need to conquer language and cultural barriers that at that point seemed too high to surmount easily. I wondered whether Chinese people would think I was "odd" for adopting a little girl from China.

In fact, if I was going to adopt internationally, choosing a child from Latin America might make more sense because I speak Spanish and enjoy aspects of Latin American culture. I'd traveled in various Spanish-speaking countries and felt comfortable with the language and food and dealing with people I'd met.

However, I had traveled to China fourteen years earlier, on a bicycle trip. So I had more exposure to China than a lot of people I knew who were also adopting from that country. Talking with friends I had begun to make who were also pursuing adoption, I learned about Families with Children from China (FCC), a support group for adoptive families. I went to one of its orientation meetings and met quite a few people in my age range who were considering adopting a Chinese child or had already done so. These connections meant a lot to me.

I began to make Chinese culture part of my life. I took a course in introductory Mandarin at The China Institute in New York City. The teacher was down-to-earth and very funny and made Chinese language and culture remarkably accessible.

I also began going to lectures and seeing even more Chinese films. But now I saw these experiences through different eyes: as the prospective mother-to-be of a girl born in China. China would become, in a way, my country.

I read some of the more popular current books about China, such as *China Wakes* and *Wild Swans*. I reread *The Joy Luck Club*, with more empathy than ever. I saw the movie and cried with a pathos coming, I think, from a growing sense of connection.

Of critical importance, I talked and visited with other families who had already adopted, from China and elsewhere. I sought out single moms in particular. A turning point came after a visit with an African-American woman who had adopted an African-American infant girl. I met her at her office. There were photos—everywhere—of her daughter and some of mother and daughter together. My eyes welled up with tears. I wanted pictures like those, too. Now I knew I was ready.

By mid-March 1996, my paperwork was complete and I was waiting for the cherished referral of a child who would become my daughter. Several months later I attended the first Chinese Culture Day organized by our local chapter of FCC. Although I felt a bit forlorn as an observer rather than a participant, I had more of an inkling of what my life was going to be like. The referral for my daughter-to-be arrived about three weeks later.

AFTER THE REFERRAL

Receiving the referral made me feel more authentic somehow, that I really would be creating a multicultural family. I became more involved in Chinese cultural events; I attended a Chinese Culture Weekend over Labor Day 1996 sponsored by The China Institute. By then I had a picture of my daughter-to-be and would show it to anyone who would look. Most of the people who attended were Chinese-American families, some spanning several generations, and I chatted with some of them about my adoption plans. I needed to talk as a way to begin building bridges.

Membership in FCC made me aware that there were many adoptive families like the one I hoped to form, and, like me, the parents were highly concerned about transmitting Chinese culture to their daughters, and were engaged in a variety of efforts to promote it. They hired Chinese-speaking baby-sitters, enrolled their children in Chinese language and culture classes, attended Chinese culture camps and festivals, helped their children's schools organize cultural activities, and did more at home to incorporate Chinese culture.

Could I do this? Yes. And I wasn't alone.

Taking Your Journey

Everyone has different needs and visions of their "family of choice." Adopting a child and creating a multicultural family is a long and complex process requiring a lot of thought, planning, and preparation. Here are a few questions to consider:

1. If you are single, what types of support networks do you have among family, friends, and organizations in your area? You may "think" you can do it all, but lining up such networks in advance of an adoption can be very helpful.

2. Have you given thought to the type of adoption you want to undertake? Have you shared your thoughts with people close to you? Will you risk alienating family and/or friends by holding to your choice? Does this matter to you? (See also Chapter 5, Confronting Prejudice . . . and Moving Beyond It.)

3. If you have a partner, do you and your spouse or partner feel the same way about a cross-cultural, interracial adoption? If there are disagreements, are you talking them through? If you don't sort these out early on, there could be problems later. Be clear that there is a consensus between the partners; your decision applies to any type of adoption, but it is especially important when you are making a move that will significantly transform the texture of your family—and will last a lifetime!

4. If you have other children, have you given thought to their reaction to adding a new sibling whose background is different from theirs? (See also Chapter 4, Creating a Multicultural Home.)

Other Stories

Following are some descriptions of how other families decided to adopt cross-culturally and how they have addressed the questions posed in the previous section.

FROM AMERICA TO ADDIS ABABA

Marsha and Luke H., philosophy professors who live in a small northeastern city, had a birth son and had already decided that if they were going to add more children to their family, they would adopt. "It seemed the right thing," says Marsha. "There are so many kids who need homes." Their son, Carl, was almost seven, and raising him had become "easy" enough that they could contemplate accommodating another child.

Once they were ready to begin the adoption process, they considered what type of child they could best provide a home for. Both full-time academics, they did not care to repeat the infant experience, and they knew that many older children were waiting for homes. They wanted a relatively healthy child who would bond with them and one who truly had no parents. This would mean, they concluded, adopting internationally.

They also realized that they would probably adopt a nonwhite child. They excluded Eastern Europe from consideration because they knew that in many cases Eastern European children placed for adoption still had living relatives. "As we read about adoption in different countries, we realized that the birth parents or birth families were still very connected to the children who were being placed," says Marsha. "We wanted to give a home to a child who would not be torn away from possible family ties." Because they already had a son, they decided they would adopt a daughter.

The H. family then examined a range of adoption literature, including the annual *Inter-Country Report on Adoption* published by International Concerns for Children (ICC) in Boulder, Colorado. The ICC report lists adoption programs for every country that has a program. The program in Ethiopia sounded right for the H. family, and the agency they contacted—the only one doing consistent and active placements from Ethiopia—had a record for arranging efficient, legitimate placements. Marsha and Luke spoke with other families who had adopted from Ethiopia through this agency. Marsha is from Chicago, where many of these adoptive families live, and these discussions influenced their decision.

Within two months of submitting their paperwork, Marsha and Luke had a photograph of their daughter-to-be, who was three years old and living in a children's home in Addis Ababa. In October 1997 Marsha traveled to Ethiopia with her mother while her husband stayed home with their son.

"She was shaking when we first met," says Marsha of her first visit with Anna, the name she had chosen for her daughter. The next day, when Marsha arrived to take her daughter with her, Anna "came and sat on my lap. I showed her a picture of Carl. I had learned a few words of Amharic and asked if she would come with me, and she said yes."

Anna is now six and thriving. Her family is part of a growing network of families who have adopted from Ethiopia and meet for an annual reunion. Many of the children, some now in their teens, remember each other from the group home they stayed in prior to being placed for adoption.

An international adoption enabled Marsha and Luke to realize their dreams of "growing" their family. But it gave them more: a connection to another culture that has been incredibly enriching for them and for their son. ("I sometimes miss being an only child," Carl admits, however.)

Furthermore, adopting a child of another race has made the H. family more sensitive to racism in their environment. "I was concerned that the organization of black social workers opposed interracial adoption, and I wanted to confront this and see how I'd respond. We thought a lot about what right we had to take Anna away from her race and culture." Moreover, the family has to deal with the fact that although Anna is African, she's not African-American, and that means addressing a different set of issues regarding racial identity. Their situation has also created bridges to other people. "When I'm out alone with Anna," says Marsha, "African-American people generally recognize that she was adopted from another place. They smile and have been helpful. They even give me advice about hair care, and they look out for her."

A LONG JOURNEY CLOSE TO HOME

In the mid-1980s, when she was in her thirties, Carla G., a single white woman, had few close friends who were parents. Single adoptive parenting was relatively rare. But one day Carla, then director of a childcare center, received a notice from a child placement agency in the city where she lives, asking for help in finding families for children needing foster care. The agency had a long list of children waiting to be placed in homes. Carla had never considered becoming a foster parent herself, but the letter intrigued her.

She called the child placement agency to say that she might be interested. The agency soon relayed the news that a healthy African-American baby boy had been born and was being surrendered for foster care. Carla agreed to take him in. Knowing he was not free for adoption, she figured the arrangement would be temporary, but it would be a good way to find out if she really wanted to be a parent. She became smitten with the little boy, whom she called Jeremy, and pursued his adoption. It became final four years later.

Living in a large city, in a middle-class apartment complex

in a racially integrated neighborhood, Carla has been able to provide a comfortable environment for her son with positive male and female role models of different races. This includes finding a Big Brother for Jeremy. Carla's parents, who are elderly and live in another state, have not been as accepting of their grandson as Carla would like. But her sister, who is an Orthodox Jew and lives in Israel, has developed a close relationship with Jeremy. He visits her for several weeks most summers.

Since Jewish communal life is important for Carla, she has become involved in a network of multiracial Jewish families, and she brings Jeremy to as many of the network's gatherings as possible. "It's so important for him to see other Jewish children like him," Carla says.

But Carla soberly reminds adoptive families to understand that "it is not easy, and there's no automatic 'happy ending' to being a multiracial family. Making things work doesn't end with finding a Big Brother or living in a multiracial building. It's a constant issue. Parents must remain vigilant at all times and for all possible situations, including some in which you might not expect problems."

HER THREE CHILDREN

Sara H. was in her early fifties when she pursued the idea of adoption seriously. Single and professionally successful, she was interested in adopting older children and possibly a sibling group. She was particularly interested in Russian adoption, since her family roots are Russian and she speaks some Russian.

The agency she chose to work with linked Sara to a sibling group of three children—two girls, eight and nine, and a boy, six. Somehow the transition from being single and childless to being single and the mother of three clicked for Sara. She had a house, a good income, a support network, and, perhaps more than anything, a determination to succeed.

In making this choice, Sara had established a solid groundwork: she had cultivated Russian-speaking friends and neighbors, obtained access to delivery services for food and other household necessities as needed, and hired household help. (She works full-time and occasionally travels.) But the "secret weapon" in the success of these adoptions, she says, was that "my kids came able to dress and feed themselves—they were already 'housebroken.' They could bathe themselves. They entertain and support each other. They have helped each other through the roughest parts of their transitions to living here. They all can cook and do many household chores. They are interesting to talk to, fun to be with, and I can't imagine my life without them." Her children are so interesting, in fact, that Sara is considering early retirement so she can spend more time with them.

A BALANCING ACT

Beth S., who is white, spent much of her professional career working in Head Start and family day-care programs in the community in which she lives. It is a racially and economically mixed (and gentrifying) area with a core of working-class Hispanic and Eastern European families, but there are also many students and young professionals who relish the area's "hipness."

When it became clear that the relationship she was in

was not going to lead to marriage and a family, Beth sought to adopt a child on her own. Her priority was to become a mother as soon as possible. She applied to an agency that was receptive to working with single people, and that had a history of placing infants within a year of the initial application. Most of the infants were Mexican-American.

Since one of her cousins many years earlier had married a man from Colombia and raised three children in Colombia, and since another cousin had adopted a child from Colombia, it was easy for Beth to envision a Hispanic adoption. Beth's extended family is quite close, so family considerations were an important part of her decision.

"I knew that my family could more easily accept a Latina child than one with African-American roots," she states candidly.

So Beth adopted an infant girl born to a Mexican-American woman in Texas. Because much of Beth's work is within the Latino community where she lives, her daughter, Jeannette, has developed many close friendships and relationships with people whose ethnic background is like hers. Jeannette still has siblinglike relationships with her former babysitter's children and grandchildren.

Recently, when Jeannette turned ten, as Beth had promised, the two took a trip together to San Antonio, Texas—their version of a homeland tour—where Jeannette was born.

COMPROMISES

Lara, who is African-American, and Ernie, who is white, were in their early forties when they married. When Lara didn't get pregnant, the couple decided to adopt. Lara was open to an African-American or biracial child, but Ernie had not resolved the loss of not being able to have a biological child, and he wanted to adopt a child who could "conceivably" have been born to him and Lara. They were matched with a young white woman who was due to give birth; the child's father was African-American. The woman gave birth to a boy, whom Lara and Ernie named Graham.

Lara and Ernie, both teachers who have second jobs, live in an upper-middle-class suburb that is mostly white but has some mixed families, and they have made sure that Graham knows other biracial children. It took a while for Lara to tell Graham that he had been adopted—she waited until he was almost five; Ernie had resisted. But when Lara and Ernie began considering a second adoption, they knew they could no longer delay telling Graham his story.

He seemed to know already, Lara says, because when she began to talk about a birth mother, Graham took it all in as though he'd heard it already somehow. She still doesn't know how he knew. Lara and Ernie have since adopted Alice, a newborn sister for Graham. Alice is also biracial.

Choosing Your Destination

Like the families I have described in this chapter, you also have decided to take the journey to forming a multicultural family. But where will you go? And how will you get there? Some people plan their trip meticulously; others simply want to form a family, and seize on the first opportunity they hear about.

Mary Wright of Montgomery, Louisiana, was less focused

on the multicultural aspect of adopting when she and her husband, Walker, adopted their daughter, Katie Yizhen, from China. Chinese adoption was the most feasible for them, considering their background and age (they were both in their forties, and Mary had grown children from a previous marriage). Multiculturalism, says Mary, isn't an issue in Montgomery, a community of just eight hundred people, with "maybe a couple of Mexicans, but otherwise just white and black—and no Asians." But after the Wrights brought Katie home, Mary began to realize that

> even though it's more comfortable to ignore the Chinese thing and the adopted thing, I began to believe that it's better for Katie to be grounded in her Chinese culture. Like tonight, just tonight, my husband said, "I just wish I could make her mine, where she's not anything other than mine." A kid at nursery school had hit her, and we asked why, and she said, "He doesn't like me." I wondered if it could be because she's Chinese. We don't know for sure, but we feel that this may happen more and more as she grows up.

For the Wrights, acknowledging that they are a multicultural family was an essential first step in helping their daughter grow up feeling more secure in who she is, in a community where there are few people who look like her or share her story. It's a journey both parents didn't expect to take *after* they got back from China, and Mary acknowledges that it's a lot of work. Just getting to meetings of Families with Children from China means driving to New Orleans, at least two hours each way. Her husband sometimes balks at it.

> I feel like all my friendships have changed, because it seems now like almost all of them are parents of Chinese children. I'll find myself talking to Chinese people I meet, in the mall, restaurant, wherever. I've made friends with a Chinese family not far from us. The mother has cut Katie's hair for a long time.

The day came when Katie Su, not yet four, waved her hand in front of her face and said that she wanted a sister who looked like her. The Wrights had already contemplated a second adoption, but with Katie Su's prompting they began to work on the necessary paperwork right away. When I interviewed the Wrights, they were waiting for a referral for a second daughter from China. Mary went to China several months later to adopt Jessica, from Shanghai.

Getting Our Priorities Straight

REDEFINING OURSELVES

You might say that all adoptive families deal with extra questions, but cross-cultural adoptions that are also cross-racial bring additional "baggage" because our children look so different from us.

It is sometimes difficult to absorb the type of permanent change we are taking on. Adopting a child whose ethnic, cultural, and racial background is different from our own requires a gritty sense of the challenges ahead. I have to admire the honesty of writer Jana Wolff, whose book, *Secret Thoughts of an Adoptive Mother*, reveals many of the insecurities she faced as she and her husband prepared to adopt a newborn whose ethnic makeup was African-American, Latino, and white.

> Back in our pre-adoption "Dark Ages," I thought race was a nonissue when it came to parenting. In fact, it is *the* issue. We have to deal with race before adoption, because it is more immediately noticeable to other people. I've evolved from an unenlightened white woman who thought all people should be treated equally, to an enlightened one, who knows they are not. And the transformation has sharpened me in ways that scare some of my friends.

Wolff has since written in *Adoptive Families* magazine that being part of a transracial family has meant having to become "more boldly public" and learning to be more creative in building a cultural framework for her family. She and her husband fear the impact of racism but sometimes also feel that they go overboard. She describes taking her son to a culture camp program, where his fondest memory is of the indoor pool and the candy he bought at lunchtime. Many parents can certainly identify!

It may be fine for us to adopt as a way to help combat racism, but in doing so, we are making choices over which our children have no control. "No one asked me what *I* thought or wanted when I was brought to the United States," says Also-Known-As founder Hollee McGinnis, who was adopted from Korea in 1975 at age three and a half. "So the important thing is that my parents gave me opportunities to make choices related to my own situation when I got older."

ADAPTING TO THE NEW FAMILY

So far, my focus has mainly been on *our* feelings as parents adopting cross-culturally and *our* ability to absorb change. But I think we need to bear in mind the feelings of children raised in an environment so unlike where they came from—and often with few or no other children like them.

Indeed, although *we* as parents may feel at ease with our adoption decision, there *are* ramifications to consider for our children. And we will need to adapt ourselves to our new life with them. Lara and Ernie, the interracial couple mentioned earlier, said that upon embarking on the adoption of a biracial child, they reviewed key issues within their daily lives as well as broader family issues. Neither set of grandparents-to-be were initially accepting of Lara and Ernie's marriage. But everyone gradually came around—more or less. Introducing the idea of a biracial child required gentle preparation and persuasion and some other adaptations in their lives.

Here are some of the changes they made:

- Believing that church membership provides an important family anchor, Lara and Ernie chose to join an Episcopal church in their area because there were a large number of interracial families in the congregation. Lara converted from Methodist to Episcopalian in the process.
- The couple bought a house in a relatively diverse neighborhood with a reputation for excellent schools.
- They got family members involved early on. Lara's mother came from another state and stayed with the

> family for several weeks to help with initial childcare. The time Lara's mother spent with the family provided welcome support and relief to the new parents and also helped her bond with both her new grandson and her son-in-law. She encouraged Lara and Ernie to consider a second adoption and offered to spend the same amount of time with a second child.

Lara's father, unfortunately, was not thrilled when his daughter married a white man, and he was lukewarm regarding the adoption. Lara's approach has been to keep a calculated distance from him. At his age, he is not likely to change, she says.

The Special Joys of Cross-Cultural Adoption

It is, of course, unfortunate when a family member, like Lara's father, will not allow him- or herself to share the joy when a child enters your family because that child's background happens to be different. But for so many families, cross-cultural adoption is a gift that not only brings love but also enriches their lives.

Lila M., a white woman married to Keith, an African-American, adopted Henry, who is multiracial. Lila, who was adopted herself, is Jewish, and Keith is Baptist, but they agreed to raise Henry as a Jew since Keith does not feel as strongly about his religious background as Lila does about hers. "We talked to him about Kwanzaa, but he wasn't interested," Keith says. The family does observe Christmas with a tree and Easter with Easter eggs, but none of the religious aspects. Henry, who is six, is learning about each parent's ethnic roots, and the family makes a point of networking with other interracial families, thus sharing many experiences and traditions they might not have learned about on their own. One unusual choice his parents have made is to have Henry begin to study French at an early age.

"We see him as an international child," Lila says. Noting that some of Henry's relatives are French, Lila and Keith have made the choice to foster in Henry an awareness of this aspect of his heritage. Henry has broadened his parents' horizons, which have been even further broadened with the arrival of Jonah, Henry's recently adopted infant brother. Like Henry, Jonah is multiracial. Families who have adopted cross-racially cannot deny how we came together. So why not celebrate? As Suzy Miller-Fuentes writes:

> One of the reasons my husband and I decided we wanted to adopt transracially is because this contributes to our vision of the world as a global community. We are extremely against racism and the countless tragedies it causes throughout the world, and although adopting interracially brings extra responsibilities and issues, we feel it is right for us. We hope to continue to further the notion of the "family of man" in all ways we can, and in addition to falling madly in love with our Chinese daughter, we know that our existence as a transracial family may open other hearts and minds. One race, the human race.

At times when being part of a multicultural family seems a bit of a burden, I take heart from the words of Mary Keen, who lives in Iowa City and is the mother of Min, adopted from China. Mary writes:

> There are so many families out there and they don't all include a mommy, a daddy, and a baby who looks like them. We are in the Midwest and this is the case.
>
> But I'm not going to ignore the fact that there will be issues to deal with (like family trees at school, and so forth). But ya know, unless you live in a small town or suburb, aren't most schools and neighborhoods experiencing this rich "mix" of backgrounds and races? This is a great time to be adopted. The world is a village.

part ii

moving forward

three

Finding Community

■

Where Our Families Live, Learn, Worship, Play—and Find Soulmates

I have a friend whose father is European American and whose mother is a Japanese national. She says when you grow up in two cultures, you aren't split in half. Instead, there are two distinct beings inside of you. If you're separate from one of the cultures, that being dies, at least for a time. It has no light to bathe in, no air, no soil. It can, like certain miraculous plants and seeds, come back to life, but the longer it dwells in that state of nonbeing, the harder it is to revive.

—*David Mura, "Reflections on My Daughter," in Half & Half*

Home Sweet Home?

When you become part of a multicultural family, you may confront issues about where to live that never occurred to you before. Now you are "different," and you may feel drawn to find a community where there are other families like yours. The advantages to making such a move are clear. If you live in a place where there are at least a few families like your own, you will have friends with whom to share concerns and activities, and your children or other family members won't feel the type of isolation and loss you or your child might experience in a more culturally homogeneous community. That's why David Mura's quote resonates with me so much.

Such considerations directly influenced Sue and Hector Badeau's decision to relocate from Vermont, where both grew up, to a Philadelphia suburb called Mt. Airy, known for its diversity. The Badeaus, a white couple in their forties, have adopted twenty children over the past eighteen years, in addition to raising two biological children. The twenty adopted children include African-American and Hispanic children born in the United States (including two large sibling groups), one son from El Salvador (a recent college graduate), two children adopted from India (although one had lived with another adoptive family before joining the Badeaus), one ethnically Chinese son, and several white children.

Although their roots and their extended family were in Vermont, the Badeaus felt that a racially and economically mixed community would be much healthier for their kids—and much more comfortable for them. Within their new community they found a church that welcomed them, as well as appropriate public school programs (including some for children with disabilities) that met the needs of their very diverse family members.

They also found an old bed-and-breakfast that they turned into the family homestead. In their case, the challenge has been to balance the many cultural needs of their children with their own beliefs. To make this work, the Badeau household has become a daily celebration of multiculturalism, beginning with the many flags that fly in front of their home announcing the presence of a small United Nations within. Mealtimes feature rotating ethnic dishes (but nothing fancy for such a large household—rice and beans, quick curried dishes, and pizza made with tomato sauce and grated mozzarella cheese on English muffins are examples). The family observes almost every ethnic holiday on the calendar in one way or another, including Chanukah, although no family member is Jewish.

"When you have a lot of kids," says Sue Badeau, "this becomes almost automatic." (In 1999 the Badeaus hosted an Albanian family from Kosovo during the crisis when some families came to the United States for a short period. In the Badeau household, adding more people just isn't that difficult, and everyone shares responsibilities.)

Certainly, living in a very mixed urban community has worked well for me. Our synagogue has become an important anchor for me and my daughter because it is an inclusive community, with adoptive, single-parent, and interracial families among its members. The congregation also includes a large number of single, childless people of different ages. Sadie and I don't stand out.

For the many single adoptive parents I've met, living in New York City has made a critical difference. Knowing other families like ours makes it much easier for us to show our children that they're not unusual. Our daughters and sons have many role models, and they need not become obsessed with the fact that they may not have live-in daddies or mommies or didn't grow in our tummies—the way some children may become if they live in a place where nontraditional families are truly in the minority.

Communities that house universities, major corporate headquarters, or hospitals tend to be quite sophisticated because they often attract top professionals from around the world. Such communities can be very adoption-friendly. Winston-Salem, North Carolina, is already a large city, and the presence of a teaching hospital has helped make Winston-Salem a "fairly cosmopolitan city, by southern standards," according to Harriet McCarthy, who lives there with her husband and three older boys the McCarthys adopted from Russia. (There are also four grown stepchildren.) Along with a family that has adopted two girls from Romania, Harriet co-runs a support group that promotes parenting and cultural issues. Among other things, the McCarthys kept their sons' Russian first names, and, she says, "no one seems to think that's strange here."

Celebrating Diverse Communities

In the course of researching my book, I heard from families all over the United States who celebrate the merits of their respective multicultural communities, and I was surprised to learn that some of them are in unexpected locations. I thought I'd share a few of them.

Minot, North Dakota? That's where Kim Breuer and her family of three biological and four adopted children (from Asia) have found a welcome mat. Kim's husband is an Air Force officer. Says Kim:

> It is very important to us that we live in an environment where we know our children will be "accepted," and I use that term loosely, perhaps, for lack of something more specific, that is to say—where we know our four youngest children won't have a multitude of problems because of their hair and skin color and the shape of their eyes.

One of the advantages to living in Minot is that it IS a military community. Here, multiracial families are so common, it's just not a big deal. You see any and all—Hispanic/African-American, African-American/Caucasian, Caucasian-Asian, Hispanic-Caucasian, and so forth. You wouldn't look twice at a mixed-race family because they're all over the place—on base and in town. While we do get second looks when we're out with our children, it's still not enough to be annoying.

The Air Force also emphasizes cultural months—Asian-Pacific Heritage month is in the spring and always a lot of fun. They also have African-American, Hispanic, and Native American Heritage months. Everyone can participate.

Our church, too, has been more than accepting of our children, who have been welcomed with open and loving arms, and the congregation really feels a part of things with our family. We have children adopted from Korea, China, Chile, and India in our church, so again, it's very commonly accepted.

Lisa Graves and her husband settled in Rowlett, Texas, a fast-growing Dallas suburb near their workplace. They always wanted to live in a diverse neighborhood, even before they had children. But they also knew that they wanted to live in a community that had good schools *and* diversity, since if they *did* adopt, it would be transracially. They now have a son, Hagen, who was adopted from the Marshall Islands.

Says Lisa:

Rowlett is an up-and-coming neighborhood that is inhabited by middle- to upper-middle-class families. When we moved here in 1994, the population was about 20,000, and we are now fast approaching 45,000. Dallas overall tends to be very segregated. There is one great neighborhood called Lakewood, but the homes are extremely pricey due to the convenience of downtown.

Of the twenty homes closest to us, we have three African-American families, two Hispanic families (with a new couple moving in next month), one Asian family, three interracial families, one lesbian-parented family, three adoptive families, four elderly families. Because my son is from the Marshall Islands, we will have difficulty finding many people with his heritage.

The downside is that there are few adult Asian/South Pacific Islanders. Most people assume Hagen is Hispanic, and I worry sometimes that this is the culture he'll link up with. Because I feel it is so important for him to know his history I am searching hard to find families with Marshallese ties. No luck yet.

The upside is that Hagen is getting strong positive views of many cultures. I personally don't want to live in a low-income neighborhood, and I want Hagen to know strong, educated, motivated, and successful people of color.

Michael Sistrunck, a single dad, lives in Long Beach, California, a city of 500,000 that is considered a "little sister" to Los Angeles. He finds this community ideal in many ways for his family: he has one foster son, who is Native American and white, and an adopted infant son, who is African-American and white. Sistrunck is African-American.

He writes:

Long Beach is a very diverse city of black, white, Vietnamese, Thai, Mexican, Central American, Chinese, Mormon, and Jewish communities all kind of woven together. There are few neighborhoods where one ethnic group predominates, and the schools reflect this diversity.

After going to school with so many different types of people for most of their lives, it makes sense that when these kids start to have kids, it is often with someone not of their own ethnicity. I love this. I think it only strengthens the character of the city and makes us work harder to support the rights of those who may not have our heritage but with whom we share a city, schools, churches, and lives.

THE BENEFITS OF A DIVERSE COMMUNITY

There are obvious benefits for you and your children to seeking out a community that is itself multicultural:

1. You will have peers who understand your situation, and your children are likely to make friends with children who share their background, so you won't stand out, and your children won't feel different or alone. In short, you won't always have to "explain" yourself or feel like an outsider. The parents you get to know may also provide resources and serve as a network.

2. Your children will more likely have access to social activities that will appeal to them, and some of these activities may become important as your children get older and experience the peer pressures of adolescence.

3. Support groups and cultural activities are more likely to be located nearby. (I know parents who have to drive for hours to reach a culture camp event or a support group meeting.)

4. Ethnic communities similar to your children's may be easily accessible.

5. Local school systems are more apt to be "clued in" to issues that you consider important. And if they're not now, there will be enough like-minded parents who can organize to address any perceived shortfalls. (For instance, another parent and I organized a unit on Chinese New Year for our daughters' preschool. The teachers were already disposed toward such an activity, but we could provide the resources. And as a nice "dividend" we had access to a high school intern who is second-generation Chinese.)

6. Resources such as multicultural nursery schools for younger children, a more diverse selection of library books for children and adults, arts and culture programs that address diversity issues, and so forth, will be easier to find.

Even if few resources are available for a particular ethnic group, if you live in a community with many adoptive families and many races, it will be easier for children of a different ethnic background to find a comfort zone.

In other cases, you may find a community with a wealth of resources—and lots of families like yours. Ellen N. moved her family to a New Jersey suburb, within commuting distance to New York City, for just that reason. She writes:

> I live in Montclair, New Jersey, well known in the New York area for its diversity. I am a single adoptive parent of two South American boys, ages six and nine. Just by way of example, my neighbors on either side are adoptive families, one ultimate "WASP" (Junior League, and so forth) with domestically adopted white kids and one Jewish father/Filipino-American mother with an adopted child who is half Hispanic, half Chinese (also domestic). Almost every class my kids have ever been in includes at least one other adopted child of a single parent. For a long time, my older boy thought all children were adopted.

But diversity was not the sole factor in Ellen's decision. She also considered Montclair's highly rated school system and the suburb's well-established Jewish community in making her choice.

THE DOWNSIDES TO DIVERSITY

There are some realities that multicultural families in urban, diverse settings may face but hesitate to discuss. In communities that are truly economically and racially diverse, the public schools may not offer the quality education we parents want for our children, nor the safe environment. In many cities, economic diversity has also created educational resegregation, with wealthier, mainly white families sending their children to private schools while public schools, attended by mainly minority children from less affluent families, remain underfunded and are sometimes downright awful.

Some public school systems now offer excellent magnet programs and are drawing the middle classes back in. In some cases, however, these programs can create a racial split within a school. This has happened in some of the "gifted and talented" programs in New York City, since they attract more affluent families who tend to be white. But it is not the case everywhere.

Carol and Daniel K. had to face this situation head-on when their first child, Jake, reached school age. The family had moved to Somerville, a small city outside of Boston known for its affordable housing and racial mix, so that they could feel comfortable as the white parents of two African-American children. But according to the couple, the neighborhood schools in Somerville

> are pretty bad, so we can't school them here. There are lots of issues about what happens to black boys when they turn eight or nine. So [Jake's] in private school. I'm not 100 percent happy with it. It's very "old money." We wanted diversity, and the school wants more kids from different backgrounds.
>
> Because of the old money, there's only superficial acceptance of diversity as a good thing. When push comes to shove, I think some people are shaken up by it. Kids like Jake get in, and some of the little blond kids are turned away. The head of admissions is doing a good job finding talented Asian and African-American kids.

An advantage of the private school as opposed to the neighborhood school is that Jake's classmates come from many backgrounds, and the academic quality is very high. But Carol and Daniel say:

> A downside for the family truly concerned with exposing their children to diversity is [that the private school] families are generally well-to-do professionals, and there's not much exposure to lower socioeconomic classes. So there's diversity and there's diversity.

Striking the balance may be difficult. Debra and Bill Berger admit to struggling with this dilemma as well in the racially mixed southern New Jersey suburb in which they are raising their daughter, Chloe, now eight, who was born in Guatemala, and their elder daughter (not adopted), now in college. Says Debra:

> We lived here nine years prior to the adoption, and at that time there were few Latin American families, so we started a support group for families with children from Latin America, and we're in the process of developing a culture camp.

For the Bergers, the flip side of racial diversity is a lack of religious diversity.

> Our elder daughter was one of two Jewish children in her entire high school. We never thought this was good, but we were not in the position to move. We always felt that it was important to live in an area that reflects your religion. Our plan was to move when Chloe started middle school. Now, we're not too sure. We think it is equally important for her to be around people with a similar ethnic background. So we have a dilemma.

Other quality-of-life problems may interfere with the search for diversity. According to Nina R., she and her husband

> moved to a diverse suburb of Seattle when we married because diversity of all kinds was a personal high value for us. Our main criteria in house hunting was finding a street with houses reflecting different incomes—big, little, new, old, different lot sizes. We soon discovered that (at least in Seattle) when you do this, you're also ensuring racial and ethnic diversity. We had no idea we'd be adopting at that point.
>
> We had a bio kid first, then adopted our multiracial child from Brazil. Three of the four families surrounding our home were interracial. We've occasionally wished we lived in one of the lovelier suburbs with less traffic. But when it comes to race, they're losers. Mostly white, a few Asians. Our street has African-American and East Indian families, multiracial families, a group home for developmentally disabled adults, a foster family (wildly fundamentalist) with six or seven kids, a family with three Asian adoptees, two with major disabilities—you get the picture. So we ignore the sound of the freeway nearby (our creek often drowns it out) and feel happy to be in these circumstances.
>
> [Yet] we had a drive-by shooting next door to our first house (one of the reasons we moved to another house nearby). But we also had a strong neighborhood group. Our kids hung out with Thai families and Korean and Filipino families, so we don't feel sorry we lived there for fourteen years. My husband says the only way he'll move out of this house is [if he is] carried [out] feet first—moving is not his favorite activity.

When Diversity Is Missing, but This Is Home

It is not always possible, for many reasons, for parents to live in a diverse community. Because of family ties or friends, parents may have deep roots to a community that does not offer much diversity or is far from a major city. And for many of us, when the chips are down or we are in the midst of a crisis, our relatives and close friends are often the first to rally around us.

Jessica Gerard, the mother of one biological daughter, Caitlin, and one daughter adopted from China, Sarah, notes that her family settled in the small city of Springfield, Missouri, because that is where her husband, a British historian (as is Jessica), was able to get a tenure-track university position in his field. But the enduring legacy of racial divisions has resulted in a highly polarized community in Springfield. The Gerards have become involved with the small Asian population there. But for multiracial families, that limited community contact (and few, if any, adoptive families) is often not enough, according to Jessica:

> After a public debate between a black woman and a white woman whose family owned her ancestors, our city organized a series of study groups about racism. Motivated by my desire to combat racism for Sarah's sake, I joined a group.
>
> Members included an elderly white Evangelical Christian minister, whose daughter had married a black man; a middle-aged white librarian, liberal, who had tested segregation in her small town with her black friends back in the 1960s; a black man whose family had lived on a farm in southwest Missouri

> for generations; and a black grandmother born in Trinidad and Tobago, who [had] immigrated with her family to England as a child and then immigrated here. One of her children had married a white person. So we mostly had interracial connections! There was also an elderly white woman raised in an interracial New York City neighborhood who seemed to have rose-colored views of race issues, telling us how everyone got on so well when she was young.
>
> I found the discussion group interesting and enlightening when I heard firsthand of the black parents' hardships in combating racism. I felt I had more in common with them, as I need to prepare Sarah for [the] racism ahead.

As the group's discussions evolved, the elderly white woman disclosed her opposition to multicultural education and affirmative action, creating serious friction within the group. Jessica found herself siding with the two black members.

> It was adopting Sarah that led to my presence there, and it was revealing to me that even if I never face racism, my beloved child certainly will in this town.

Families such as the Gerards recognize both the strengths and the shortcomings in their situation and have had to find different solutions.

THE SMALL-TOWN ADVANTAGE

Despite the diverse cultural offerings in many cities, you may, quite simply, love where you live: you may cherish the countryside, with the advantages that come from having space and being in beautiful natural surroundings that are also likely to be child-friendly. But there are drawbacks. A mother in a rural community commented that opportunities to pursue the cultural roots of families like hers—she has adopted children from Korea and China—remain as limited today as they were more than twenty years ago, when she first adopted.

Yet she loves the warmth her family has received in

> small-town America: They've been wonderful to my kids, taken great interest in them, been supportive to our family in many ways.

By living in a rural community, you may lose a certain anonymity that is part of life in urban areas—but you will gain the personal contacts and caring that often come with settling in a small, close community.

Similarly, Nancy M., the mother of four young children adopted from Brazil, reports:

> Although our area lacks diversity, we also have a close-knit community where everyone knows everyone and is very interconnected. In my mind, their difference makes our children special and known in a positive way. (When they get to be the age of dating, perhaps things will change, I am told.)

But in such a setting, parents have to be extra vigilant. Nancy adds:

> Although I know that hate crimes can occur anywhere, we try to be at least aware of where the hotbeds are by reading and

subscribing to publications such as those of the Southern Poverty Law Center. (We did this before the children also, but now it has new meaning for us.)

One day I was referring to one of my employees whom the children knew as being adopted. My oldest daughter looked at me in exasperation and said, "Mom, almost everyone is adopted!"—like, why is that important? I hope that it is because we have provided her with a healthy adoption community.

Elana Hanson, the mother of two daughters adopted from China, was living in a very small town when she and her husband embarked on their first adoption. Elana made the small-town ambiance work in her favor.

We were in a sort of bedroom community to Colorado Springs, with lots of ranchers. It's basically a white community, with maybe one Chinese family who own the local restaurant, and maybe two African-American families, one member a high school coach. So I thought this might not be a really friendly community for an Asian child. What I did was just start hitting all the local businesses, most of whom at least knew my face from living there for ten years, and talking to merchants and workers, anyone who would listen, about our coming adoption.

I was rewarded with interest like I never expected. As we waited sixteen months while China rewrote its adoption laws, every time I entered a store someone asked about the progress. I called the little weekly paper, and they followed my story and put an article in the paper after our daughter arrived.

Sixty-five women from my little mountain interdenominational church responded with a baby shower, and all but about four were retired and grandmothers. I also called the Colorado Springs paper, and they did a story as well. The editor even ended up adopting from China!

Where I expected prejudice and unkindness I found only acceptance and excitement. I even appeared on a local TV show to answer questions. I certainly was never a publicity hound before, but in order to pave the way for my daughter's acceptance, I put aside my shyness, and now I talk to groups anytime I have the opportunity to tell our story.

DRAWBACKS OF SMALL-TOWN LIFE

Although there are many positive aspects of small-town living, it may eventually lose its charm for your family. The community closeness that was quite appealing when you have very young children may become less relevant when children reach school age. Elana Hanson's family relocated to Colorado Springs, a city of 500,000, following the adoption of a second daughter. Although the Hansons relocated for professional reasons, there were important family benefits. They found a racially mixed neighborhood, schools more suitable for their daughters, a sizeable community of adoptive families, and a large number of families from China and Taiwan. The Chinese community in Colorado Springs runs a language school and sponsors many Chinese cultural activities that the Hansons attend. Being in a larger city also made it easier for the Hansons to find a church suited to their beliefs and needs as a diverse family.

Similarly, Alice and Tom E. decided to relocate from the all-white, semirural community they'd been living in to a larger community closer to the city, where they knew they could find role models and peers for their two young adopted African-American children. Alice says:

> This year we moved closer to the city, in a search for a more diverse neighborhood. It is important to us that our children see other people, especially kids, who look like them. As for problems [being a multiracial family], our current community doesn't seem to care much, or maybe [the people] are too polite to say anything, other than a few stares at the grocery store or the occasional curious comment. In that sense we benefit from the rural mind-set; farmers hate to be intrusive or impolite. Our daughter's day care/preschool has a few multicultural families, which helped break the ice when we enrolled her there. But finding any ethnic hair care products for her has been nearly impossible, so I usually shop for those kinds of things in the city.

Indeed, such special "excursions" are sometimes necessary to preserving your children's awareness of their cultural background if you cannot relocate your family to a more diverse area. To some extent, families living far from a major metropolitan area are stuck in the same cultural void most families experienced many years earlier when very little was going on to recognize multiculturalism. While many products and services can be accessed via the Internet, that doesn't make up for the lack of direct contact. Says one mother:

> It's hard to keep cultural heritage going in rural areas like ours, where there are no culture classes or language schools. And we need to drive most of the day to get to activities that apply

> to our family. We can't do it often enough for my children to feel connected, so when we do, it becomes a "nice" experience, but it is only that.

While she relies on catalogs and occasional urban excursions to fulfill the children's cultural needs, this mother says, "I'd give anything for a chance to take my kids to a church that reflects their background."

AN ADOPTEE REFLECTS

So far I've only discussed the choices parents make regarding the communities in which they choose to raise their children. But what can the *children* tell us? Listen to Kirstin Nelson, the biracial adoptee whom I mentioned in Chapter 1. She grew up in rural Nebraska.

> When I was little I didn't think much about the fact that I was the only black child in my grade school . . . and my junior high . . . and my high school. As I got older I became confused and resentful that I had been deprived of living around people who look like me. I still struggle with this issue today. I now live in a very diverse city and I will never again live in a predominately white or rural area. Nor would I ever consider raising my children in such an environment.

Nelson was twenty-six years old and in graduate school when she made her first close friendship with a black woman. She sorely regrets not having been able to make such a friendship earlier in her life. By not growing up in a diverse community, she says:

I missed out on so many valuable experiences—the kind that would have shaped my view of the world and the very essence of who I am. I love my parents very much, but I disagree with some of the decisions they made when I was a child. They did what they thought was right, but unfortunately they didn't have the resources to help them understand all the issues that are involved in transracial adoption.

How You Can Help Create a Diverse "Community"

Here is a list of strategies for families who don't have easy access to cultural resources in their communities.

1. *"Stretch" yourself to find organizations that will meet your children's cultural needs.* Membership in adoption support groups is helpful, but it's not always enough. Judy Thorpe recalls the day when her daughter, who was almost three, told her, "When I grow up I will be white like you, Mommy."

> When I said, "No, honey, you will always have your beautiful brown skin," she began to cry.
>
> I knew then that we weren't doing enough. Interacting with other cross-culturally adoptive families was not enough. We immediately became much more active in activities that included many different adults and families of a variety of ethnic and racial groups. As our children are South Asian, we joined the Indian Association and became active participants. We are fortunate that we live in a university town, so it is

> easy to join in various multicultural activities and programs through the university.
>
> Now that my children are all teens, I can look back and say that each of them was different while growing up. One of my daughters began coming home from school complaining that she was the only one in her class who had brown skin. She begged to change schools; and when we found just the right one for her, she just blossomed and was very happy there.

2. *Provide images in your home of role models representing your children's background if they won't encounter such role models in their daily environment.* A mother of two African-American children suggests creating collages using photographs of people whose ethnic background reflects that of your children.

3. *Be proactive.* Help your children's teachers understand your concerns, and offer the school books and other resources as educational aids. You may—following Elana Hanson's model—also want to launch a mini-public relations campaign to prepare friends and neighbors for the arrival of your child.

   If you have older cross-culturally adopted children, your task will be even harder. Even in more diverse communities, school systems and other community institutions are often not prepared to work with families with adopted children, even under the best circumstances. Schools and other institutions, such as hospitals, may be prepared to work with immigrant families, for instance, because there may be a large number of children of particular ethnicities in the community. But the needs and histories of adopted children are different and specific. You will have to be your children's strongest advocate and ensure that school officials—principals, teachers, district administrators, and special educators—understand your situation.

The parents of two youngsters adopted from Kazakhstan, an eight-year-old girl and a ten-year-old boy, observed that their son was being ostracized at school because he was different—he was struggling with learning English and not understanding American classroom dynamics. He also had difficulties with his studies. (His younger sister was not being ostracized in the same way.) The boy's mother was furious—she and her husband had been misled about the school's offerings to meet her son's needs—and she realized that she could take nothing for granted from then on.

The mother offers this advice to other parents who find themselves in a similar situation:

> Ask yourself, "What will the teachers and school do to ensure a smooth entry for my child into the school?" (You will probably have to suggest things like a classroom buddy and/or a homework buddy to help your child understand what is expected, a lunchtime buddy to explain the cafeteria system, a gym buddy to help explain rules, and so on.) Figure out how you will know what is happening in the classroom and how your child is adjusting. For example, you could set up a system of notes, e-mail, or conferences in person and by phone so

> you will be in the loop, at least for the first few months.

This mother's efforts are impressive. But it is important not to idealize the experiences of families who have sparked change in their communities. It can be hard, frustrating work.

4. *Take part in culture camp activities that focus on your children's background.* Getting there may involve some travel—but it may also be fun. Providing your child a once- or twice-yearly exposure to his or her birth culture is certainly better than offering nothing at all—or doing it all long-distance. And whether or not your children are actively engaged in the cultural activities themselves, they will have the opportunity to meet children like themselves (and you'll meet parents like you).

   Says one mother:

   > We had the pleasure of attending the West Coast reunion of families who have adopted from Brazil. It was great for both us as parents and for our children. At their age, they seemed to have few questions about those around them and were interested only in playing hard. The sharing that went on was wonderful.

   For the children, culture camps or family affinity networks can be critical. The mother of an African-American boy cites the family's participation in a multicultural Jewish family network as an essential activity. "It's important for Jason to know that there are other children like him," she says. (See the listings for culture camps in Chapter 8, Goods and Services.)

5. *If there is a university near where you live, find out if there's an international students association, and if any members come from your child's birth country.* These organizations often sponsor cultural events that are open to the public. You may also be able to connect with student group members who might come to your home and may perhaps be "big brothers" or "big sisters" to your children. One woman I know located such an organization to find a Russian student who would help translate for the eight-year-old Russian girl she had adopted, and who later served as a tutor for the child.

6. *If you're on-line, join a discussion group of families like yours.* Such groups are increasingly easy to find through Web sites such as *eGroups.com, Go.com*, and *Parentsoup.com*. Through these sites you can find listings of adoption discussions that will probably fit your own niche. You can also create your own discussion group. America Online hosts dozens of adoption discussion groups and offers a thorough adoption resource that includes archives of earlier adoption discussions.

   The Internet is an essential tool for adoption networking. I recommend to any parent who has not yet done so to learn how to use a modem. If you have a child in upper grade school, you can ask him or her to show you how!

7. *Locate pen pals for your children when they're old enough. Adoptive Families* magazine often lists requests for pen pals in its letters column. Now that so many kids are computer-literate, you may also seek "electronic" pen pals for your children.

A NOTE ON FINDING COMMUNITY WHEN YOU ADOPT OLDER CHILDREN

Parents adopting older children from another culture face a special challenge to make their children feel welcome and integrated into their community. From the beginning, parents have to be prepared for a period of culture shock and adjustment, and they need to be very patient. It is best to work closely with schools, neighbors, and institutions that are important in your life so that you can establish a framework to welcome—but not overwhelm—your child.

You may want to cut your child some slack because she may need to go through a grieving process (which may be very private and not obvious to you) before she is ready to plunge into the new environment called home. On an e-mail discussion group, one mother of many adopted children reported frustration when, four months after coming into her new home, her newly adopted thirteen-year-old daughter from Asia refused to do housework (although the other children in the house shared chores) and refused to do schoolwork (she had a very light load adapted to her need to learn English and other basic skills). Other parents weighing in on this e-mail discussion group advised the mother not to get too worried; but they suggested setting limits on the time the teenage daughter could spend in front of the television, and offering positive, concrete reinforcement for doing chores and schoolwork.

This advice came from an e-mail discussion group established especially for families who have adopted older children, and many of the parents had already dealt with similar issues. This reassurance helped the mother know that she wasn't alone, and that there were workable strategies for addressing her situation. The mother has gone out of her way to help her daughter meet other older adopted children from the same country. And several months later she reported that her daughter had become actively engaged in school, family life, and their community.

FINDING A SPECIAL FRIEND FOR YOUR CHILD

In some cases, it may be useful to find people in your community who speak your child's language, and perhaps ask one of them to become your child's "special friend." There is a transition period when your child is absorbing a whole new set of stimuli and slowly losing much of his or her birth language and cultural memories, which can be a painful, isolating, and traumatic experience. Offering your child a way to maintain a connection with his or her language and culture through another person—a university student, for instance—can be invaluable in many ways, helping your child feel that he or she is not alone.

If you are interested in adopting an older child, you may want to consider adopting a sibling group, or you may want to plan a second adoption of an older child from the same background. Martha and Allan Reading (who have adult children from previous marriages) first adopted Emma when she was seven, and then Annie at age five and a half, when Emma had turned nine. Both girls are from China. Their companionship enables them to share common cultural roots and memories and also not to feel isolated as they adapt to a new family and a new life.

four

Creating a Multicultural Home

■

Cultural History, Religion, Role Models, Language, and Family Trees

My husband and I just adopted a little biracial infant. We are Caucasian. We live on a small farm, and we both have had experience with minorities to some extent through our teaching experiences (Navajo and Mexican-Americans). Our little boy is part African-American. We don't want to miss out on sharing his heritage with him in any way. We have some books already (but they are for an older child). Are there any recommendations for while he is an infant? We live in a farming community.

—*a mother in Indiana*

I don't think we can give our daughters a Chinese upbringing like they would have had in China. Not just because we are not Chinese, but also because this is not China. But we do have to realize that children absorb their culture from their parents by the way things are done.

I know that a Christmas tree goes up in December and there are gifts, cookies, visits from relatives, cookies, decorating, cards, more cookies, Mass, cookies, dinner, and EVEN MORE COOKIES! Only Mass has to do with the religious aspect of the holiday; the rest is my culture. [We even learn] to put on makeup by watching our mothers, TV, and advertisements. What will my daughter's idea of beauty be when most faces are Caucasian with blue eyes and blond hair (that describes me).

We intend to give her a card on the anniversary of her adoption telling her of the love and happiness she has brought us, and give her a gift from China (jewelry, silk, and other items). Her birthday will be all-American. Lunar new year is a time for family, and at the start we will light a candle for my husband's ancestors, one for mine, and one for hers.

We will send her to Sunday-afternoon Chinese school. Food will be Chinese and American. We will take her back to China when she is older. Of course, there are museums, shows, and other things here that have Chinese culture, but I want to expose her to more than just Chinese (and American).

I just feel strongly about this. One of my Chinese friends said I'll know more about China than she does at this rate.

—an adoptive mom

Many parents who adopt children from countries outside the United States "fall in love" with that child's birth culture. They go so far as to take language courses, learn to cook that country's traditional dishes, attend cultural summer camps. Adoption of these children offers parents an exciting new exposure and immersion that they would not otherwise have. But I would caution these parents not to lose sight of their own family culture, their neighborhood culture, their national culture. Family ties and identity come first—they provide love, stability, security. Substitution of another culture is a social experiment that threatens to fragment our children's identities. Children are not vehicles to take us on a world tour.

—*Terry Cox-Joseph,*
"The Care and Feeding of a Multicultural Glutton,"
Roots and Wings *magazine,*
January 2000

Building Cultural Bridges

One of the biggest challenges we face when we raise children whose background is different from our own is striking a balance between our birth culture and theirs. Although we're not officially obligated to maintain our children's birth culture, many adoptive families choose to do so in one way or another, so that our children have a better sense of their total being. It is a long-term investment in our children's sense of self, because as they grow up and are less "protected" by us, some people they meet will make assumptions based on first impressions—what they look like rather than who they are.

And our children will be better off if they know "who" they are, because then they will be better prepared to respond. Susan Soon-Keum Cox, an adoptee and an adoption professional, says parents should make it their

> priority to respect both the dignity of the child's birth country, as well as the dignity of the child. Whenever a country supports intercountry adoption as a way for a child to have a family, they are giving a great deal. A nation's decision as a matter of policy to permit intercountry adoption of its homeless children is not an easy one for any country. They do have the right to define the system as they feel it should be.

So how do we do it? And where do we begin? Is it possible, in fact, to have a "multicultural" family?

Some folks say no. They reject the "multicultural" label because, as one father asserts:

> A family has a single culture. It may be an admixture of a number of practices gleaned from several cultures, but it is a single culture. For most of us (at least those living in North America), it is virtually impossible to teach Chinese or Vietnamese culture. Culture, by definition, is something that must be absorbed over a long period of time. I daresay that those Occidentals among us cannot even fathom what it means to be from an Eastern culture. We may observe Tet or the Autumn Festival, but we're going through the motions. The underpinnings derived by living in Asia for extended periods (that is, since birth) are simply absent. Moreover, our Western culture permeates all that we do, even if the trappings of what we do contain elements of practices from other cultures.
>
> That is not to say, however, that we cannot honor our children's heritage. It is by incorporating elements of the cele-

> brations of their homelands that our children will come to understand something of the land of their birth. The fact remains, however, that our children are or are becoming Americans or Canadians or Britishers or whatever, and it is in our cultures that our children must live. I want to make sure they are good at it.

I disagree with some of this father's statements: I believe a family can be made up of several different cultures without "consolidating" the family into one. He and I both recognize and celebrate the diversity of our families instead of ignoring it, but we also acknowledge our limitations. We just express our beliefs a bit differently. At the home of Hector and Sue Badeau, being multicultural can even have a witty twist. Sue describes a seminar on teenage adoption at which her African-American daughter, Renée, was a featured speaker. Renée was adopted at age sixteen; she is now twenty-eight.

> After Renée spoke, the first question *wasn't* "How does it feel to be adopted as a teen?," but "How does it feel to be adopted by white parents?" Renée said, "My parents aren't white." Then she paused. "My father is French Canadian and my mother is Spanish and Italian. And we celebrate *all* the holidays!"

Sadly, some parents are somewhat scornful of their children's birthright, for a range of reasons. People who make statements such as "My child is American, and that's that," which I hear most often, seem to be giving no further thought to what the implications of this attitude will be for their child's self-esteem if his or her birth heritage is ignored or, even worse, derided. Such ignorance can be harmful. One mother recalls:

> [I attended] a reunion of six families who traveled together to China to adopt our daughters, and I was disturbed to hear their hostile and negative comments about China. They denigrated the country as dirty and smelly, condemned the medical system, and blamed the orphanage for the poor health of their children. One little girl had bad memories, even though adopted at eight months, of being tied down hands and feet, and is terrified of Chinese people, music, and so forth.
>
> I feel the parents eagerly reinforce this fear by their own distaste for the Chinese. Several of the parents were quite paranoid, not wanting information about their children to be included in the book a returning mom presented to the orphanage recently. They are very ethnocentric, and I do wonder what their views will do to their little girls over time. [The child's father] and I kept quiet about our views for [our daughter] Sarah's sake. So I guess we are not as typical [in engaging with the Chinese community in our city for our family's sake] as I had assumed.

BALANCING CULTURES AT HOME

Some parents make a conscious effort to incorporate their children's birth culture into the routine at home. Some hire nannies who speak the language of their child's birth country. Others send their children to day-care centers or schools geared to the child's ethnic background. Some parents may choose at some point to spend several months or longer in the child's birth country, sometimes taking jobs teaching English, for example, as a way to share a unique experience and develop closer ties to the country. Lisa McClure, the Denver-based single mom of a four-year-old from China, took a teaching job in China, planning to stay up to two years, because she felt, above all, that it was important to learn to feel totally comfortable around Chinese people. (She has also created a Web site about her experience.) She observes that many adoptive parents don't extend themselves this far, and that breaching this particular culture gap was critical for her family. Encouraging our children to know and feel good about where they come from may also ease the way for them to explore their roots if they so choose.

Sometimes we pursue this "culture quest" because of our own interest, not necessarily our child's. Connie P., who lives in a neighborhood of Queens, New York, which has a high Chinese population, told me:

> Our home has changed quite a lot [since the adoption]. Ping has been attending Chinese preschool since age two and is now fully bilingual. I always saw incorporating her birth culture into our home as far more important than any of our cultural tidbits. My husband and I have forsaken the religions we were brought up in—he's Catholic, I'm Jewish—and are studying Buddhism. We attend a Buddhist temple on Sundays, complete with a vegetarian lunch. The group is very racially mixed, the majority being Chinese. We observe Xmas as a nonreligious holiday (Xmas is quite popular in the Chinese community). We have a kitchen god in our kitchen to which we feed sweet things. I have become accomplished at cooking Asian dishes and can shop with the best of them at Hong Kong Plaza. In fact, most of our diet is Asian. Our daughter

> eats almost no dairy but lots of soy and sesame oil. I have been studying Mandarin for three years, and I continue to struggle. Right now my reading and writing are ahead of my speaking. We have never called our daughter by her English name, but she does know it. I changed my name legally and took a Chinese middle name. Our daughter knows she is Chinese and is very proud of it; she is able to distinguish Asians from Caucasians. This is as far as we have gotten, but as she gets older I plan on going further into my daughter's birth culture.

I personally prefer to seek a greater balance between my birth culture and my daughter's. Neither Connie nor her husband (who have since adopted a second daughter from China) maintain strong ties to their roots. They are naturally drawn to Asian culture, and they live in a neighborhood that has a high percentage of Asian families and many Asian resources. Ping was not yet three when Connie spoke to me about her life with Ping. Will Connie's Chinese studies continue as Ping gets older? And what happens if Ping decides to focus on English-only when she's in school? Will her schoolmates do the same? Connie equivocates and wonders whether Ping and her new sister will hold on to their Chinese—and if as their mother she is doing the right thing in the first place.

"You're American, *we're* American," admonishes Joy Kim Lieberthal, who was adopted from Korea at age six, and who finds the culture overload inappropriate for many children. Our goal, ultimately, should be to find a balance as we seek to impart our culture to our children, but at the same time we also seek to instill in them a sense of pride and self-confidence in their unique identities.

But we need to be careful. Ultimately, it's up to our children to decide when—and if—they wish to pursue their birth culture. Hollee McGinnis, for one, did not take Korean culture seriously until she was in college and made her first trip to Korea when she was twenty-four. "I wasn't ready until then," she told me. Similarly, she began to study Korean only when she really *wanted* to learn it. Tackling a trip to Korea *or* the language just wouldn't have worked when she was younger, she says; the visit would have been too confusing, and she admits, "I know I wouldn't have done my homework!"

Indeed, trying to force a child to develop an interest in another culture, especially through travel, may backfire if the child or young adult isn't open to it. But how, I asked her, can we parents know when to push cultural learning and when to ease off a bit? Was I doing the right thing to take Sadie to Chinese language and dance classes? Was she losing out by *not* having a baby-sitter who spoke Chinese?

"You should make the culture available so she knows about it," Hollee said. "But don't force it at a time when she doesn't want it, and don't go overboard." On the topic of baby-sitters, Hollee had a more pronounced opinion: "Choosing a nanny because she's Chinese is race-based—and not necessarily in your child's interest." Food for thought. I've sometimes regretted not having a Chinese baby-sitter for my daughter, because I think Sadie could have developed a nice relationship with the right one.

MAKING A COMMITMENT TO YOUR CHILD'S CULTURE

The adoption process sometimes requires new adoptive parents to become familiar with their child's birth culture and to agree to sustain it within the home. In Chinese adoptions, for instance, parents must write a letter to Chinese officials (under the auspices of the agency they are using) saying why they want to adopt a child from China. Then, in China, during interviews with provincial officials to finalize the adoption, parents are asked to describe how they plan to promote their child's Chinese roots. Thus, becoming somewhat educated about Chinese culture and history helps.

Similarly, families adopting cross-racially in the United States are also often asked by court officials, as part of the finalization process, how they will help their children develop a positive sense of their racial identity.

Yet unless they receive advance counseling on this topic, from their agency or a home study writer, or do their own research, many parents do not prepare for the actual change in their lives that occurs with a cross-cultural or interracial adoption. Many don't consider it important or simply don't anticipate it. Author Jana Wolff notes:

> We knew we wanted a healthy newborn, but we didn't feel a strong need to be matched by race or features. Our willingness to parent a child of a different race had more to do with naïveté than with altruism. We weren't sufficiently aware of the repercussions of adopting transracially to have been proactive advocates for that option. We didn't understand that we might be taking on a job even bigger than parenting—that of transmitting a culture that was not ours. We simply knew that we wanted a baby, we believed that we would be good parents, and we presumed we could love in any color.

As Wolff writes, she and her husband have had to learn—on the job, as it were—how racial issues pervade the life of a child of color. As parents, they confront this reality in various ways whenever they are with their multiracial son. Their son will confront it always.

There are different approaches to learning about and incorporating our children's culture into our home lives. Five areas I explore here are

1. cultural history and traditions,
2. religious observance,
3. role models and mentors,
4. language, and
5. the family tree.

Promoting Cultural History and Traditions

Most families have access to plenty of materials to help them learn about other cultures and traditions, and more sources are coming on the market every year. (See Chapters 7 and 8.) But there's certainly nothing like having firsthand experience, either through the communities you live in, schools and after-school programs, or, if necessary or appropriate, culture camps or homeland visits. In some ways, it's easier for families that adopt internationally (depending, of course, on our access to resources) because our children's geographic difference lends itself to an array of activities.

The promotion of culture in families formed by interracial adoptions within the United States can become more complex because of the legacy of racism. (Some would-be parents still report encountering difficulties with local agencies when they seek to adopt children of different races, despite federal legislation designed to encourage interracial adoptions as well as several studies showing that such adoptions do not harm children's self-esteem.)

A white couple who participate on an e-mail list I subscribe to asked for advice as they prepared for a hearing to finalize the adoption of their infant son, who is African-American. The social worker who was assisting the couple with the adoption informed them that the judge presiding at the hearing would want to see that the family had a plan for giving their young son a sense of his birth culture.

One mother, Lorie Anderson, replied with the following excellent list, which I have paraphrased. You should be able to adapt her guidelines to meet your family's needs.

1. *Enable your child to interact with other African-American people, branching out to diversify your circle of friends and acquaintances (not just other families that have adopted transracially).* Doing this may seem contrived at times, and you might have to reach beyond your own comfort level by becoming more outgoing. It might mean traveling to a black church or a black neighborhood, joining a black cultural association if there is one, whatever it takes. Some people relocate in order to live in a more diverse area. Some people send their kids to a summer camp where they can meet other black kids (or at least not just white kids). Author Jana Wolff (*Secret Thoughts of an Adoptive Mother*) wrote about trading homes with a family for some summers so that she and her husband could give

their son the experience of living in a black community.

2. *Plan to consult with your black friends on hair styles and hair care and skin care.* Also get their advice on cultural considerations and recognizing, understanding, and coping with racism.

3. *Plan to learn about black history and the black experience and be prepared to teach this material to your child—and not as a separate topic, but integrated as a natural part of his or her education throughout the year.* Plan to become an expert. Give yourself a self-taught course in black history, or take a college course. Continue to subscribe to on-line discussions to stay informed about issues and ideas. Plan to subscribe to magazines that target African-American readers, such as *Jet, Ebony, Raising Black Children*, and *American Legacy*.

4. *Plan to celebrate black holidays and special events and the lives and history of famous black people—Kwanzaa, Martin Luther King Jr. Day, Juneteenth, Black History Month, and others.*

5. *Plan to buy black dolls and children's books and videos that show black people who are not just token representatives.* Lorie's family often listens to *Gullah Gullah* (a television program on Nickelodeon) and music videos. Plan to tune in to television programs that show black people in nonstereotyped ways, and tune out those that tend to stereotype. Plan to tune out television programs that don't show any black children.

6. *Reflect the beauty of the African-American culture in your home and in the experiences that you provide to your child.* Lorie's family loved the African Children's Choir when they visited their area. Visiting cities where there are African-American cultural events and exhibits is a must for them because they live in a small, mostly white town.

7. *Plan to seek out and use black (or at least nonwhite) professionals in your area so that your child can experience black role models; this is especially important if you live in a predominantly white area.* This sounds terribly race-conscious, but your child shouldn't have to grow up thinking that all experts are white.

8. *Plan to talk to your child about racism, how it could affect him or her, and how to respond to it.* Plan to prepare your child with strategies to address racism, and plan to intervene to whatever extent possible when racism does occur in the family, in the community, at school, on the way to school, wherever. I hate to include racism on a list of black culture suggestions, but I do think it's an integral part of black history and culture.

9. *Plan to try to convey a balanced approach to all of this so that your child doesn't get too focused on being black, but rather gets a sense of being a human being with an African and African-American experience and heritage.*

A key element to this plan is for adoptive parents to show respect for our children's birth culture, even if we don't know a lot about it—now—and to be willing to venture into our children's culture, however alien it may feel at first. If you do it right, this process won't feel strange for long, and your circle of friends and overall perspective will widen considerably.

You certainly don't have to wait until you have your child to start preparing. Linda Kingston, who was awaiting a referral from Guatemala, shared some of her ideas on how she plans to lay the groundwork for a multicultural home:

> I want to volunteer at an organization that supports Latino causes and have my children raise money for charities in Guatemala. We will sponsor a child in Guatemala, host an exchange student from Guatemala, and encourage our children to go to Guatemala as exchange students themselves. I would like them to speak Spanish fluently and I plan to hire a tutor when they are in preschool. I do speak some Spanish, and I want to work on becoming fluent.
>
> I plan to spend time with them learning about Guatemalan history, culture, holidays, geography, economy, and so forth. I want them to understand whatever they need to know in order to feel comfortable there. I know this is impossible to do completely because we live in the United States and I am white, but I will do my best.

I think of myself as an "ongoing learner" with regard to Chinese culture. In a real sense, Sadie and I are in it together. She certainly has a lot more "ownership" of it than I ever will, but for now she will get information about her culture only if I make sure she does.

HOMELAND VISITS

Tours to an adopted child's birth country are becoming increasingly popular, and some adoption agencies as well as independent groups are organizing more each year. Information on these trips is published in adoption magazines and sometimes on-line. Some adoption experts say that for a first tour your child should be between the ages of eight and twelve; others feel children should be at least in their mid-teens—or older—to benefit from the experience.

During the summer of 1999, Anne Russ, a college professor, and her thirteen-year-old daughter, Dorinne, joined a two-week tour of adoptive families visiting Peru organized by the Ties Program (see Chapter 8, Goods and Services). Dorinne told me that she didn't want to go "because I was going to miss my boyfriend and didn't want to leave him for two weeks. I used to go crazy if I didn't talk to him for an hour! But I had no choice. My mother made me go."

Most of the families on the trip had children younger than Dorinne, and just one child was her age. The memories she related to me included long lines at the airport at customs, searching for luggage, the poverty in "scummy" Lima (where she had been born), the fancy hotel where she and her mother stayed, and the trek up Machu Picchu, near the city of Cuzco. Only Dorinne and the other girl her age made it to the top of the peak. And Dorinne says she was the only one who didn't get sick.

Adopted at three months, Dorinne, who lives in upstate New York, said that she feels no connection to Peru. She describes herself as a typical teenager who likes to "go to the mall, hang out with friends, and talk on the phone." Although she says she speaks some Spanish, she said her trip did not bring her any closer to her Peruvian roots—yet she is glad she went. As for "looking different," Dorinne admits that some people assume that she's "Indian" because of her olive skin, but with her hair dyed red with brown streaks, others think she has a dark tan.

Some adult adoptees I've spoken to believe that adoptees should take a homeland trip only when they are old enough to absorb all the complexities—and that adoptees should make the trip on their own, because it is a very personal journey. In the case of two adoptees I spoke to, they made their first trips when they were in their twenties, even though their families offered such a trip when they were younger. This is, of course, a judgment call, and you can make this decision based on your own child's interests and what you think he or she may be able to get from such a trip.

Judi Kloper, an adoptive mother of three young adult children from India and a little girl from China, and the biological mother of a son, describes the trip she took to India with her then teenage daughter:

> Our older sons from India have no desire to return, though at some point I will take them. However, our daughter, who arrived at nine years old (twelve years ago—she's twenty-one now) very much wanted to return for a visit. I told her that when she was sixteen, in tenth grade, the year that they studied India, I would take her back. And away we went. It was awesome, but difficult in some ways, as she came face-to-face with a visual explanation of why she might have been in an orphanage, what her life could have been like.
>
> She then went back in 1998 to volunteer in two orphan-

> ages in a different part of India. I believe that while overall it was beneficial for her in so many ways, it was also too much. She was nineteen at that time. She found that she didn't quite fit in. She didn't quite fit in in America, and she didn't quite fit in in India. However, she is definitely proud to be Indian, and definitely happy to be American.
>
> I have many friends who have taken their younger children back to India at ages seven to ten, and all did well. They absorb different things at that age than what they would at, say, age sixteen or twenty.

For some adoptees the homeland trip can have a dramatic impact. Judi describes the experience of a young man adopted from Korea who now coordinates national culture camp programs for a major adoption agency:

> He spoke about how he hadn't wanted anything to do with his Korean heritage, though his parents tried and tried to incorporate it into their lives, and tried to interest him in it. When he graduated from high school, he had fully intended to go to Mexico or somewhere similar with all his buddies. His parents told him that he couldn't go, and that he was going on a homeland tour of Korea instead. He went, and he spoke of what a life-changing experience that was. He came home to the United States with a different view of things. He ended up working for an adoption agency and has a real passion for it.

For some adoptive families, the "homeland" visit could be to the city in the United States where your child was born. Even if you adopted your child as a newborn, he or she still has connections to that place. One mother took such a trip with her ten-year-old daughter to San Antonio, Texas, her daughter's birthplace. Upon their return, she reported:

> We live in a culturally and racially diverse area in Queens, New York, where I think my daughter really feels at home. She never really talked about being a person of color (she is Mexican-American). But in her hometown of San Antonio, she was one of the majority, not just part of the rainbow of her school.
>
> We saw the courthouse where the adoption was finalized. She learned some history, gained a clearer understanding of what it means to have Mexican ancestry even though she was born in the United States, and absolutely inhaled the spicy Tex-Mex foods. She was very eager to identify herself with San Antonio.
>
> At our visit to the adoption agency, my daughter sat quietly while I spoke with the agency representatives. The person who had escorted her to New York, whom we wanted to see the most, wasn't present, but we were able to ask questions. My daughter asked, "Was I in this room?" and when she was told that yes, she was there during the transition to and from foster care, she looked incredulous. Her current self had come in contact with her past, with those five days which we know nothing about. She didn't seem to connect this statement with the fact that her birth mother had been there—but I did. It was quite emotional, to say the least.

Sometimes we need to let our kids alone. The father of a boy adopted from El Salvador noticed his son surfing on the Internet one afternoon looking at sites related to that country. He decided not to comment. Since the boy had not previously expressed interest in El Salvador, the father decided to let his son have his own private journey.

SETTLING ON THE BEST NAME FOR YOUR CHILD

Using first or middle names that reflect children's background is a common strategy, especially if the children are older and have lived with a certain first name for many years. Some families may choose to give their children a first name that reflects their origins if their last name does not. Keeping the birth name or giving the children another name from their birth culture can reinforce a pride in their ethnic identity.

Most of the children Sue and Hector Badeau adopted were older, so they had already "owned" first names for a long time. But José, their son from El Salvador, was just two and a half years old when he joined the family; Raj, who was born in India, was only six months old when he was adopted. José's name was on his papers, so the Badeaus kept it. When the Badeaus adopted Raj, the orphanage sent a suggested list of Indian names, with translations, asking the family to consider choosing one of them, and so they did. "I feel strongly about keeping names that reflect our children's culture. It's one of the few links they have with their past," says Sue.

I named my daughter after a beloved grandmother but kept her Chinese name as her middle name. She knows that her middle name is the name she had when I adopted her. Other parents I know have either kept the names their daughters came with as their first names or chosen other Chinese names based on research they've done to find a name they felt would suit their child.

There may be times when a child's given name may present a dilemma for the adoptive family. When I was writing this book I knew a Jewish family that was in the process of adopting a four-year-old boy from Bulgaria whose first name was Christofer. Feeling uncomfortable with that name, the family chose a different first name for him with a similar sound.

With other children, changing names may be difficult, but your children will be the guides. One family who came back with an eight-year-old boy from China describes their experience:

> While in China we called Noah by his Chinese name, not wanting any confusion on anyone's part over names being used compared with paperwork. We continued to call him Lu Lin for a couple of weeks after returning home.
>
> One day when he was asking about names, the time seemed right to tell him he would have a new name here, keeping his Chinese name as his middle name, and introduce him to his whole "new" name, using our names as examples. He seemed quite pleased, although [he continued] to refer to himself as Lu Lin for another three or four days.
>
> Then he referred to himself as Noah Lu Lin for several days, and finally he felt comfortable enough with the whole thing to call himself Noah! There was no rush in doing this, and we watched him make that change, one of many.

Other families may feel uncomfortable using a first name from their child's birth country. One mother I know gave both of her Chinese-born daughters complete American names, saying that the other names were "orphanage" names and had no real meaning to the girls. Some children may want an American name. (It is customary in many Chinese-American families to give the children English and Chinese names, and for the children to use the English names outside their homes.)

Our children are often wiser than we think when it comes to dealing with "outsiders'" expectations of a certain ethnic name matching a racial or ethnic type. As a result, we grown-ups are forced to change our own preconceptions of the naming dilemma (and of what it means to "look" Chinese, Jewish, Latino, or whatever). In one case, I asked a young Korean-born man, who has a common Jewish surname, if he ever felt uncomfortable with it. What a mistake on my part. "That's my name," he said bluntly, "and that's who I am. Why should I want it any other way?"

Hollee McGinnis, founder of Also-Known-As, put it more directly: "I *love* being McGinnis!" she told me. (Her first name is a combination of an English and a Korean name.)

There are times when a child may not want to keep his or her birth name. I had assumed that older children especially might want at least a portion of their name to be preserved. I learned otherwise.

Debby Ramundo observes that one of her sons, adopted from Vietnam at age seven, "wanted very much to change his name":

> I kept his Vietnamese name as his middle name and gave him a new first name. He insisted on using his new name in Vietnam for about a year before he came home, and to this day he does not want his Vietnamese name on anything. He had a fit

> that it was put on his new birth certificate and citizenship papers. He wants to assimilate; he does not want to stand out and be different.

GETTING SIBLINGS INVOLVED

Families with two or more children face an interesting challenge with regard to cultural involvement. The bottom line here is one simple word: inclusion. Get all the kids involved in the various activities that reflect your children's different backgrounds. If not all are interested, that's fine. But don't leave anyone out.

The mother of two daughters, one biological and one adopted from China, explains her family's approach:

> The way we see it is that we are a Chinese-American family now, we are bicultural, and the whole family should participate in celebrating Chinese culture. We want to avoid the classic "Why are all the Chinese objects in *my* room?" situation, where only the adopted child is associated with her culture.

So this woman's eleven-year-old biological daughter has studied Chinese. When the family attends Chinese events, she, her mother, and her Chinese-born sister wear traditional outfits. It is important to remember, however, that this family—and yours—has firm roots of its own that also should be preserved and honored. (If you're a Chinese-American family that has adopted, the story is different.) This mother adds:

> I realize that we are not actually ever going to be really Chinese, and that Sarah will be raised in the mainstream Ameri-

> can culture and its values. The books, toys, decorations, food at home are pretty superficial, and teach a heritage, not a daily all-embracing culture. But I feel that it has been good for our elder daughter to share the experience of learning about her sister's Chinese heritage.

A special challenge for some parents is how to help children who were adopted at an older age feel that they are on an equal footing in the family with children who were born to their parents or adopted as newborns. Children who were adopted when older may feel a sense of loss at not having any documents, photographs, or artifacts from their babyhood. MaryBeth Lambe is the mother of two children adopted from China, one at age five and the other at age two. (MaryBeth and her husband, Mark Levy, also have three biological children, one foster child, and an African-American daughter, now eight, who joined the family at age two months.) MaryBeth says:

> A big issue for our older kids is that they don't have baby pictures of themselves—and that kind of makes them mad. To make up for this sense of loss—especially since we had baby pictures of the other children—we got lots of pictures of babies from China and told them to pretend these were their baby pictures. They'll say that these are our "pretend" pictures—maybe that's what I looked like.

This strategy clearly doesn't make up for the genuine loss the children feel. But it represents an effort to connect the children to where they came from and to give them a sense of parity with their siblings. MaryBeth's children have responded in a positive and realistic way to their challenges as members of a multiracial, multicultural family.

Deciding About Religious Observance

Adoption experts concur that children should be raised according to the adoptive parents' religious traditions, because these represent the true home life and offer stability and consistency. But families who are religiously observant may want to consider ways to modify their approach to incorporate the concerns and background of their adopted child. When there is no religious tradition at home, parents can create nonreligious celebrations that suit their particular styles and incorporate their children's birth culture.

But what if there is no religious tradition at home, and your child's culture is strongly faith-based? What if the parents themselves represent more than one faith?

Here are some possible strategies:

1. *Find a house of worship that provides a middle ground that can accommodate a family with more than one cultural and religious tradition.* I know families who have joined Episcopal or Unitarian churches that, to them, represented a satisfactory compromise.

2. *Attend a church whose membership represents the children's ethnicity.* This strategy is particularly useful for two types of families:

    · those families with African-American children, for whom participation in church activities may help generate friendships and cultural connections to the community; and

- those families with children adopted at an older age for whom the ethnic connection can be very meaningful. This was the choice made by Carol and Steven Forslind, the parents of five children adopted from China who joined the family at ages ranging from four to twelve; as of this writing, the children now range in age from eight to fourteen. (The Forslinds are also parents of eight biological children, now grown.) The family located a Chinese church in their New Hampshire community, and Carol and Steve are the only non-Chinese there.

3. *Seek a congregation whose membership is more diverse and/or accepting of families that are interracial, interfaith, and so on.* I've been fortunate, as a Jew, to find a synagogue that welcomes families like mine.

Although there are various solutions—and you must find the one that suits your family best—perhaps an ultimate goal is to create a "hybrid" culture. For that reason, I was intrigued by a fascinating article I read in *Adoptive Families* magazine (December 1998) that described a holiday called "Kwanzukaa," which combines the ethics, rituals, and values of Chanukah and Kwanzaa, for families whose members are Jewish and African-American.

Similarly, families that follow Judeo-Christian traditions may want to incorporate aspects of Hinduism or Buddhism into their homes, as a way to acknowledge these religious traditions in their children's birth cultures. Doing so does not mean that you need to convert, and there are ways to combine the traditions creatively. Visits to Buddhist monasteries or Hindu temples are a great introduction. Books on different ethnic holidays, such as *Kids Around the World Celebrate!*, by Lynda Jones, provide easy family craft projects and recipes that can help make other cultures accessible (see Chapter 7, Publications).

One family chose to customize a Kwanzaa celebration to meet the particular needs of the household:

> For the past three years we have been crafting a Kwanzaa celebration in our family. We don't celebrate throughout the seven days; instead, we focus only on the last day of the Kwanzaa celebration (December 31). What we've found is that our kids have such a rollicking good time that they much prefer a Kwanzaa fest over a New Year's Eve bash, which suits me just fine.
>
> We have a small collection of children's books, which we read during the day; we do crafts from those books; we decorate the dining room with black, red, and green crepe streamers; use a length of African-design fabric for a tablecloth; create the centerpiece with the traditional symbols; and celebrate with an evening feast. Before eating, we light the *kinara* (a candleholder). As the kids light each candle, we say, "*Habari gani?*" ("What's the news?") and read a short passage explaining which of the seven principles that candle is being lit for.
>
> Then we feast on sweet potato pie, cornbread, garlicky collards, black-eyed pea salad, and chunks of fruit dipped in melted chocolate for dessert (not sure that the last is standard Karume fare, but it kind of drives home the idea that Kwanzaa

means "First Fruits"). Then we adjourn to the living room, put on some music for Kwanzaa (plus an occasional reggae), and play games or dance.

The first year it felt a little stilted, but not anymore. But then, I'm a big believer in families crafting traditional celebrations like this, and we do this a lot throughout the year. It pulls the family together (and I always use some kind of special meal with traditional foods to center the celebration on!), and it's a fantastic way for kids to live out and appreciate their own, or someone else's, heritage.

We also celebrate Chanukah and Christmas and highlight the ideas of miracles, faith, hope, love, and compassion that each holiday represents. My theory is that if children can live out such meaningful celebrations of not only their own heritage and culture but others as well, they will come to value and respect the beliefs of others; and the process of dismantling racism, prejudice, and religious intolerance will begin.

Finding Role Models and Mentors

Role models are critical for our children, to give them a sense of pride and possibility and not being "unique"—in a negative way—as an adopted child. I'm lucky to live in a community with many families like mine, including many headed by single parents, so although my daughter sometimes expresses the desire to have a daddy, she knows her family situation isn't unusual.

Doctors, clergy, police officers, school principals, shop owners, and other people in authority influence how our children see the world. We can seek out professionals with the same background as our children's in an effort to reinforce a sense of ethnic self-esteem, confidence, accessibility, and equality—and the potential to succeed.

A new development in the adoption community is the formation of mentor programs. The group Also-Known-As launched an initiative in 1999 to provide mentors (older adoptees) for younger Korean adoptees. The original goal was to create one-on-one relationships between older and younger adoptees, but there were not enough older volunteers, so the program was modified to match a mentor with a small group. Culture camps offer similar role models, because the camps generally recruit their counselors from among older adoptees from the same ethnic background as the campers.

Other role models may be young adults whose background is the same as our children's. So, for instance, you may try to find a Big Brother or Big Sister whose race and/or ethnicity is the same as your child's, particularly if you're living in a community where such role models may be difficult to find in the course of normal activities. (The downside is that such programs often have long waiting lists. The African-American son of a single white woman was on such a list for years, and was ultimately matched with a young white man. That relationship has been a very committed one, and the mother says that it was more important that her son have a consistent male role model than that he find someone of the same race who would give him dedicated time, so she and her son are delighted with his Big Brother.)

Mary Pickard, who lives in St. Paul, Minnesota, says that finding a mentor made a huge difference for her ten-year-old son, John, who was born in Paraguay.

At the Resource Center for the Americas in their community, the Pickards met a Uruguayan man who plays Paraguayan harp. Although the man, who was in his late twenties when they first met, normally doesn't teach harp, he agreed to take John as one of only two students. Initially, their friendship was short-lived: the man was preparing to move back to South America, and Mary bought one of his harps for John as a memento.

But the teacher later moved back to St. Paul, and John resumed lessons with him. The lessons enabled John to have a special connection to his birthplace and also to feel special about himself. John's growing sense of accomplishment with the Paraguayan harp helped build his self-esteem.

Role models can also be sought out in more informal settings. In an e-mail discussion on tending to the hair care of African-American children (an important topic for families who adopt black children), one mother said that she preferred to cut her son's hair at home, because it was more convenient, less expensive, and she had gotten good at it. But another mother suggested that investing in a professional barber was worthwhile for other reasons. She wrote:

> I don't blame you for wanting to save money, hassle, time, and so forth, by cutting your son's hair at home. But you might want to visit the barber shop now and then anyway for reasons beyond a haircut: Your little kid gets to know and become friends with black adults who can end up caring about him and providing resources for him over time. He will learn about being a black male from other black males. This experience can also be a great bridge for you to other events, people, and activities in the black community.

My daughter Sadie once spotted a police officer who, she said to me (suddenly becoming quite shy), looked like he was Chinese, and I asked her if she wanted to say hello. She nodded. He was the commanding officer of a police station within the New York City subway system, and his office was annexed to the station. He turned out to be of Chinese-Cuban descent and was delighted to talk with Sadie. He took us on a tour of the station and let Sadie wear his cap and hold his walkie-talkie. Of course I had my camera! These types of encounters can demystify the gulfs between children and authority figures and also reinforce a sense of ethnic pride and accessibility. (See page 136.)

Role models are also essential for parents (and parents-to-be). I was encouraged to pursue an international, intercultural adoption because I saw so many people with backgrounds similar to mine who were doing it and deriving so much satisfaction from being adoptive parents. I attended several events hosted by Families with Children from China while I was still making up my mind about adopting and while I was waiting for my referral. I also took an introductory course in Mandarin.

It was critical for me to see other single parents who had adopted from China, not only to know that it could be done, but to know that I would have a support network to draw on. As an older parent, I also appreciated seeing older parents coping with issues that I would surely confront along the way. I knew that there were also problems—many of us are not as spry in our forties and fifties as we were in our twenties and thirties—but I was reassured hearing many of these parents say that they felt they were doing a better job as older parents than they would have if they had started raising children at an earlier age. Many of them were well-established professionally and felt very happy to be raising children at a time when quite a few of their friends were sending their own children to college.

Addressing Language Issues

The heritage of most children adopted across cultures, especially internationally, usually includes a different language. In the past, adoptive parents generally left that language behind, unless they happened to speak it. And the children, including those who were adopted at an older age, tended to jump right into learning English. How many of us know families—adoptive or not—in which parents who speak a different language try desperately to encourage their children to learn the language by speaking it to them all the time—and the kids answer in English? Many of these children see themselves as American—full stop—and they just want to fit in. And that means speaking English.

Nowadays, speaking several languages is seen as such an asset that many primary schools, particularly in ethnically diverse communities, now offer second-language instruction and so-called "dual language" programs in which children are taught in two languages. Students in such programs can be children with a birth language other than English or children for whom English is their first language. Both types of students profit from learning in two languages. (My daughter attends a kindergarten that is taught in English and Spanish.) And families who wish to emphasize their child's birth language have a plethora of resources to choose from: audiocassettes with workbooks, videos and computer programs, culture camp activities, and "Mommy and Me" classes that target mixed families. For adoptive families, bilingualism may not be the goal as much as helping our children find a comfort level with their birth language in the event that they choose to study it in greater depth when they are older.

In researching language resources for this book, I heard much more from the Chinese adoption community (and not just because I'm part of it). There are several reasons. First, in recent years the number of Chinese adoptions has soared. Second, the size of the Chinese immigrant community throughout the United States has grown tremendously, and with it has come the establishment of Chinese culture schools. And Mandarin and Cantonese, unlike many other languages spoken by children adopted cross-culturally, require special instruction to teach tones and characters. Because the Chinese dialects do not have common roots with English, as do the Romance languages, learning Chinese is a more intense experience.

In general, there seem to be three common-sense questions to consider regarding pursuing a second language program for your child:

1. How committed are *you* to the second language? Are you willing to take classes on your own or with your child?

2. Are you sure your child is interested in learning another language and has the aptitude? Some children may find coping with two languages too confusing—and some may not want to take on the instruction or may not be ready for it.

3. What is your goal? Do you want your child to be bilingual, or will you be happy if your child has a basic grasp and appreciation of his or her birth language?

HELPING YOUNGER CHILDREN KEEP THEIR BIRTH LANGUAGE

Roberta F., a single mother, adopted twenty-three-month-old Juliette from China. Juliette already spoke "toddler" Mandarin. By chance, Roberta found a terrific shared childcare arrangement close to home with a Mandarin-speaking nanny who was already looking after two older girls who had also been adopted from China. Although Roberta had not planned to focus on Juliette's Mandarin, she realized that if Juliette was exposed to Mandarin every day, she would probably keep it, even if Roberta couldn't help her speak the language at home.

When the two older girls entered full-day kindergarten and the caregiver found other employment, Roberta enrolled her daughter at a day-care program in New York City's Chinatown, in a Mandarin-speaking classroom. According to Roberta, as a result of her daughter's previous experience, Juliette is the only child in the class who is completely bilingual.

Says Roberta:

> I am very gratified that this all worked out. All along I never placed exposure to Chinese-Americans and Chinese language as my top priority, but we fell into these wonderful arrangements. It is good to know that she will always have the tools to communicate with people who look like her. She has already started talking about her "Chinese mommy," and I think it's

> very possible that she will have some issues to work out about how it is that she became an American and her departure from the land of her birth. I think that her ability to speak Chinese and her comfort with other Chinese-Americans can only help when she grows up and lives her life as a citizen of the world.

WHEN YOUR CHILDREN ARE OLDER

Martha and Allan Reading, parents of two daughters adopted (at different times) from China at ages five and seven (girls who are now seven and ten), wanted their daughters to retain their Mandarin, and so they enrolled the girls in an after-school Chinese culture and language program located in a community with a large Chinese population. Martha also takes Mandarin classes. She writes:

> Chinese Culture School is not for everyone. But I feel that our older girls should retain as much of their native language as possible. Some people say that if we send them to Chinese Culture School they can't be "all-American." What is "all-American" anyway? Wonder bread? I feel that it is important to help our adopted Chinese children appreciate and learn about their birth country. This does not mean they have to be scholars on China; it just means they learn at least as much about China as they learn about Europe in school.
>
> One thing that I have learned from the Korean adoptees is that no matter what we might try to do to help our kids feel and be seen as "all-American," they will encounter people who will not regard them in the same way. I want to make sure that

my Emma and Annie can proudly say, "I was born in China, and I am an American now!" I think they can do that only if they have been exposed in a deliberate way to their heritage.

Parents of older adopted children are often amazed at how quickly their children pick up their new language and lose the one they were born speaking. But more is lost than we may realize when children make a transition to a language structure and context that may be vastly different from their original one.

As described in Chapter 2, Marsha and Luke H. adopted Anna from Ethiopia when she was three. The child was six when we met. Marsha recalls:

> Anna's transition to English was very fast. The only words from Amharic that she uses are the ones that we have retained and use—even though we learned them from her initially. When Ethiopian adults speak Amharic to her now, she gets a bit panicky and isn't sure whether she understands. But last spring she did tell her name to a man we met who asked her in Amharic what her name was. She did it almost spontaneously before she was aware of what she was doing. Similarly, the last time she had a shot at the doctor's office, she was very scared, and as the doctor came toward her with the needle, she grabbed me and said something in Amharic. Shots are a particularly traumatic memory for her since they are associated with her arrival at an orphanage about eight months before she came to us.

Although Amharic isn't a language Marsha's daughter has many opportunities to use, Marsha feels it's important for

Anna to maintain her birth language in some form. Says Marsha:

> My mother, who is a child psychologist, tells me that one's first language remains the "language of emotion." To us, the loss of our daughter's first language (or at least one of her first—she may have learned Amharic or a new dialect of it when she first came to the orphanage) is just a symbol of the loss of her Ethiopian heritage. We do as much as we can to keep that legacy alive for her, although it is impossible to make it a central structure of her experience.

I agree with Marsha's assertion that the loss of cultural heritage is one aspect of the international adoption process. But we shouldn't see only loss; adoption is a way of *responding* to loss and giving children new hopes and opportunities. By giving our children access to other cultural traditions—in Marsha's family's case this includes Jewish traditions and, more generally, American ones—our children do attain a rich and rounded life. The family is making the effort to keep Anna connected to her heritage. They eat Ethiopian food, meet Ethiopians when they can, read books on Ethiopia, and are active in a network of families who have adopted children from Ethiopia. This network meets annually in the Chicago area, where many of the families live.

Sharon Puttmann's daughter, Carla, was adopted from Guatemala at age seven. Despite many attempts to save Carla's Spanish—speaking the language at home and spending time with Puttmann's sister and brother-in-law, who speak Spanish fluently (and who adopted a daughter from Peru years before Sharon adopted Carla)—Carla lost her ability to speak the language. Sharon says:

> She really wanted to let it go. There were many bad memories of her life in Guatemala, and the language issue was intertwined with these memories. Before she had been here a year, she spoke no Spanish and understood very little. She didn't want to hear it. She didn't want it spoken around here.

Six years later Carla began studying Spanish in school and picked it up very quickly. She clearly had retained memories of Spanish syntax and pronunciation. Now highly motivated, she is doing well and enjoying the language. And that, Sharon says, is key.

Children's degree of mastery of a language ultimately will depend on how motivated they are to learn the language. One mother quipped that her teenage daughter would love to be able to speak and read Korean, "but she would like to learn by magic." Hollee McGinnis of Also-Known-As says that she became particularly motivated to learn Korean when she began preparing for her first trip to Korea. The Korean adoption community is increasingly promoting Korean language courses for older adoptees who plan to visit or work in Korea—or just want to grow closer to their birth culture.

Carol and Steven Forslind of New Hampshire adopted their five children from China at ages when all were already talking. The youngest was four at the time of adoption, and Stephen, the oldest, and the most recently adopted, was eleven when he joined the Forslinds in August 1999. Two of his new sisters were young teenagers at the time.

Carol writes:

> The two youngest children lost their Chinese within three months, but the older children have kept their birth language. The two older girls and our new son use Chinese at home. I have had to go to Chinese school with the two younger girls, and they are picking it up very fast, much faster than I am. The fact that we use Chinese at home has helped. Our new son doesn't use any English at home, just in school, and they say that he is doing very well, but I don't know because he refuses to speak English at home. Stephen is quiet and doesn't want to make mistakes.

The older girls had stopped using Chinese at home about a year and a half prior to the family's trip to China to adopt Stephen, even though they continued to attend Chinese school. The girls had insisted that they were *not* going to be able to understand the language well enough to talk to anyone in China, but, Carol says:

> Once we got there, they started using Chinese and didn't stop talking the whole time we were there. They had thought that they wouldn't be able to communicate. Wrong, they had the best time, yakking their way across China.

One year after Stephen joined the Forslinds, Carol reports:

> Stephen still will not use English at home. He will play games with the younger girls, and they understand him but answer in

> English. The older girls use Chinese most of the time at home. I cannot believe how much I understand. Chinese school has been good for me too.

Sara H., a single mom of three children adopted from Russia at ages six, eight, and nine, commented nine months after their arrival:

> My three kids [adopted in a sibling group] have retained their Russian . . . They are just now beginning to show signs of losing some of their facility (they forget words in Russian or mix a lot of English into a Russian sentence). Lately I have had to remind them more often to speak Russian and not English. I am functional enough in Russian that we only speak Russian at home, and I am about to start private Russian tutoring for myself in an attempt to improve my Russian to the point where I can handle more complex subjects.
>
> My kids also have a Russian-speaking baby-sitter, go to a Russian-speaking therapist, and go twice a week to a wonderful Russian theater class. We rent Russian videos all the time and will soon have two channels of Russian TV via satellite.
>
> My kids are in a bilingual (English/Hebrew) setting at school and are learning both languages well. My oldest speaks the best English and the worst Hebrew, my middle kid the best Hebrew and the worst English, and my youngest is okay in both. I hope that they will retain enough Russian so they can regain it later if they want, but I know that it will be increasingly difficult, especially since I am not a fluent native speaker. I'm sure it helps that they have each other to speak to in Russian.

For all her effort, Sara cannot guarantee that her children will keep their Russian. Sara admits:

> Another girl we know about the age of my middle child who was adopted at the same time has already lost all her ability to speak Russian, although she still understands a little. Russian friends of mine who speak only Russian at home say that after about three years, their kids stopped answering them in Russian even though they still understand. I feel lucky that my kids are still speaking Russian after nine months.

CAUGHT IN THE BREACH

We should not take our older children's rapid language acquisition for granted. They may seem to speak English fluently in a matter of months, but they may not pick up the nuances and complexities of verb forms and pronouns that might have been structured differently in their birth language.

Also, trying to find a suitable academic environment for our children can be very tricky. We may not ever know precisely what type of learning our children had before they joined us or the teaching style they were exposed to. The problems Martha Reading's older Chinese-born daughter, Emma, experienced could certainly be parallel to those of other children adopted from other countries.

Martha writes:

> Because Emma's spoken English was so excellent and her vocabulary grew so fast, we were all fooled into thinking that she understood more than she really did and that learning to read would not be difficult. Wrong! Now it is obvious that Emma

does not have the language foundation to do well, and she is struggling with reading comprehension.

Plus, our Chinese-speaking children have to learn that English requires tenses, plurals, grammar usage, which Chinese language does not require. I believe that it is neither how well our children speak English nor how large a vocabulary they've developed that is key to reading comprehension, but it is understanding the nuances of the language, the colloquialisms and the cultural definitions and interpretations of words and phrases. English is a very difficult language because of these factors.

Reading recommends that parents become aggressively involved in their children's education from the outset, including pressuring schools for one-on-one English-language tutoring both to give children a kick-start and to help them feel secure. As parents, we need not only to encourage our children through the transition, but also to be alert and prepared for the need to provide them extra support.

Laura and Jackson A. adopted two Russian-speaking youngsters at the same time from Kazakhstan who were eight and ten when they arrived in the United States. Prior to their arrival, Laura visited a number of district schools and chose one that she believed would be most supportive of her children. Her eight-year-old daughter made a relatively smooth transition, but her ten-year-old son, Nicholas, had a rocky time. Not speaking his new language well, combined with being teased by his peers, having a teacher with an inflexible teaching style, and being assigned academic work that was more difficult than what he had done in Kazakhstan, made the boy anxious and depressed.

> We made the mistake of requesting a teacher who had a reputation for being "structured" and "in control" of her classroom because that is what Nicholas was used to in Kazakhstan. It was a mistake because what he really needed was compassion and empathy—not a rigid academic environment. He was going through so many new things that learning all the "rules" in that classroom was too much for him and he shut down.

Based on that experience, Laura offers the following advice to parents who might find themselves in a similar situation:

1. Find out how the English-as-a-second-language program functions in your school. (Is the program classroom-based, or do the children attend special sessions?)
2. Explore whether the school has experience with children who have been adopted at older ages or if the school's experience is limited to serving the children of immigrants. (If the latter is the case, you may want to suggest resources and talk to teachers, guidance counselors, and, if necessary, the school principal about specific concerns related to the adoption.)
3. Work with the teacher from day one to assess your child's academic ability and performance. It may be appropriate to put your child in a younger age group to start. Ask how the school will determine your child's academic level, and request that an interpreter be identified as soon as possible.

4. Find out what options you have in terms of classroom assignment, and then meet with other parents in your child's grade to find out about the personalities and teaching styles of different teachers.

5. Talk to your social worker and other parents with children who have been adopted at an older age to find out what type of classroom environment is best.

Ultimately, Laura moved Nicholas to a school that had smaller classes, in-class support for English-as-a-second-language, and a volunteer-run after-school program to help children with their homework. The new school worked with her to create a more appropriate and individualized program for Nicholas so that he could learn without being frustrated. Looking back, Laura feels that she could have done more by meeting parents of Nicholas's schoolmates-to-be—except that after settling on one school, the family had made a last-minute decision to place him in a different one, so there was no time to make the necessary inquiries.

THE LANGUAGE PARADOX

For some adoptees, learning the language of their birth country as a way to affirm their identity just isn't important to them, and we must allow them that leeway. Sue Badeau recalls the dilemma her Salvadoran son, José, faced when he entered college and joined the Latin American student association on campus. There was enormous pressure for him to identify with a particular Latino group—would he align himself with Salvadoran students, or with another group? José didn't want any of this. For him, being Salvadoran didn't carry more weight than the combined English-French-German-Italian background of his parents. Although he had studied Spanish, he was not fluent.

Furthermore, as the result of his interest in computers and martial arts, José found he had more affinity with campus groups dominated by Asian-Americans. Ultimately, José left the Latin American group to do his own thing, including joining an Asian-American student group on campus.

The Challenge of Family Trees

At some point, most of our children will come back from school with a homework assignment many adoptive families dread: the family tree! Although genealogy discussions are not a concern specifically of multicultural adoptive families, they can affect us more acutely because they further emphasize that our adopted children had different birth parents and cultural roots.

What type of tree would reflect our families? Or does it have to be a tree? Could we create a family "orchard" or a special type of bush—or a garden? And how do you create such a chart when, in the case of some adoptions, you know nothing about the birth family?

"I'm still waiting for ideas about how to do a family tree incorporating adoption," writes Elana Hanson, the mother of two girls adopted from China, "especially since we have NO information about our children except their city (maybe) and real birth date" (information that few adoptive parents of children from China have, unless, as is occasionally the case, a note was pinned on the child when he or she was abandoned). Elana suggests having a tree trunk represent the child, and setting up big branches for the parents, "and then little branches off those for all the other relatives."

Another parent recommends a three-branched approach—or as many as it takes. One branch is Mom's side, one is the father's (in a two-parent family), and one is the birth family.

Another family, with daughters from China and India, has come up with this model: the roots of the tree represent each daughter's birth culture, including birth parents, foster family, and orphanage caregivers; the daughters are the trunk; and the parents are the branches. An alternative is to scrap the tree altogether and create a family "wheel" with the child (or children) at the hub and the family members all around.

One adoptee asks why the family tree is so ubiquitous and places so much emphasis on genetics, especially at a time when families are changing so much. Raised in a closed adoption situation, she had no information on her birth family and happily listed her adoptive family in tree projects as she grew up. She suggests replacing the family tree project with a "more open-ended assignment allowing the child to structure it in his or her own way," with titles such as "Things that are important about my family" and "Things people in my family remember from the past," which enable a child to present a project that accurately—and richly—portrays the adoptive family.

Another adoptee, Martha Osborne, who edits the on-line adoption magazine *RainbowKids* and has adopted four children (three from China, one from Korea), angrily recalls the family tree project a beloved aunt presented to her clan:

I am a thick-skinned person, but my mouth dropped open when I came to my own "branch" and saw the word "adopted" printed under my name. It was like a slap since it seemed to say, "not a REAL blood member." I am really close to this aunt and uncle, so I asked her if she thought that was important. I mean, I am either family or I am not family. Part of the tree or not. Who cares how I got here. Why make this distinction?

She said, "Well, I mean, you are family, but you know . . . I mean," and it was written in her face. I am family, but I am also not REAL family in her opinion. Luckily, she seems to be the only one who feels that way, but still it was a shock, knowing how incredibly close we all are, that she would feel that her own children (and she tried to explain this to me) have a blood tie, which, of course, I should understand is deeper than an adoptive tie. I just said, "Wow, and all this time I thought you were my real aunt. Guess I was very wrong about that." We finished up the family dinner and nothing more was said, but I was smugly glad when I discovered that my mom left my aunt's family tree "gift" behind as well.

part iii

meeting challenges

five

Confronting Prejudice . . . and Moving Beyond It

Sad to say, LOTS of prejudice still exists here and now, although we have had less trouble since we moved to [an urban area] from [a semirural area]. My responses to folks who display prejudice, stereotyping, and ignorance with regard to race ranges from ignoring them to educating to responding rudely, depending on the situation. If people can see your children as individuals and you as their forever parents, they are usually worth keeping in your life.

—a white mother of two African-American children

I would suggest to anyone who has not had the opportunity to take a diversity workshop to do so. As a Caucasian I can tell you it is a growth experience and one that I think can help anyone begin to learn what it means to be a person of color in this country. Our children are people of color, and we should grab at any opportunity to better understand what they will have to deal with as they grow up in the United States.

—Martha Reading, mother of Emma, ten (adopted from China at age seven); and Annie, seven (adopted from China at age five)

An Ugly Reality: Prejudice and Stereotyping

One way or another, prejudice often insinuates itself into the lives of multicultural families. It can be insidious—the media love to latch on to negative aspects of adoption—and it can hurt our children. If you haven't experienced prejudice yourself, it can come as a shock once you've adopted a child of another race.

The white mother of a six-year-old black boy reports that adoption totally changed her understanding of racism:

> I used to oppose it on principle; now it's personal. When I am alone with my son, I am treated very differently than I am treated when I am either by myself, with my husband, or even with our whole family. The assumption when I am alone is that I am involved (or have been involved) with a black man and I am treated as inferior. There are stores that require ID for my check when I am with my son but not when I am by myself. I've been followed by store security. I understand just a bit of what my son will face as a black man, but most important I understand that it's only a small piece of what will be his experience.

Sometimes the things people say to us or the way they treat us may seem innocuous and well-meaning. For instance, people will tell me how cute Sadie is (and, of course, she is; I *am* her mom!). But then I get the feeling that they're not saying it because she's my daughter and she's cute, but because she's my adopted Chinese daughter, and this makes us different. Sometimes I sense that people bend over backward in their comments because they don't quite see us as a "whole" family (in part because I am single), or as a "real" family, or as individuals. A first cousin of mine, meeting Sadie for the first time, told me how cute Asian babies are—as if Sadie were someone else's daughter, and not *her* (second) cousin.

The "nice" comments people make can be harmful, even if they aim, superficially, to frame our families in a positive light. Stereotypes—for example, that a child will do well in math and science because of her Asian genes—represent a form of prejudice. They strip the child of her individuality—and they take away her freedom to define herself based on her gifts and predilections.

Like friends of mine who report having similar experiences, I would often shrug and smile at many such comments when Sadie was still quite young. As our children get older, however, we need to be more thoughtful about hearing what people say and responding appropriately, in ways that address our children's needs, especially if people are making assumptions about our children that have nothing to do with who they are as individuals.

Sometimes (too often, in my view) negative presumptions are made about cross-culturally adopted children. This generally happens in tandem with negative media on adoption—stories about one ill or violent child from a certain region are interpreted as evidence of a problem endemic to all children of that child's ethnicity. Cross-racial adoption—usually white parents adopting African-American children—can provoke more pronounced incidents of prejudice, both as a result of a basic prejudice and because of an abiding concern within some factions of the black community (and formally articulated by the National Association of Black Social Workers, as

I discussed earlier) that cross-racial adoption constitutes a form of "racial genocide" in the United States.

In fact, several highly regarded studies of cross-racial adoptees have indicated that children of one race placed with parents of another do as well emotionally and developmentally as their counterparts raised in same-race families. United States legislation now bans discriminating against prospective adoptive parents on the basis of race, although cases of discrimination have been reported by white parents seeking to adopt black or biracial children. (In a highly publicized case in St. Louis, the black aunt of a biracial girl sued to annul her adoption by a white couple and to win the right to raise the child herself. Since the child's father, the aunt's brother, had never been involved with the child and never indicated interest, the court turned the aunt down.)

The potential for prejudice, no matter its source or degree, puts demands on parents to be prepared to intervene and to be proactive. There *are* some real strategies.

Cheri Register, the mother of two daughters from Korea, addresses many of these issues in "*Are Those Kids Yours?*", one of the first books to explore international adoption in depth. She reviews the types of attitudes adoptive families may face, and she suggests bearing in mind that our first obligation is to protect our children, not to educate the rest of the world. Although some questions people ask about our children or their adoptions may be well meaning, they serve to separate our families from others, and we need to be selective about how—and when—we respond.

Families that include children who are African-American or biracial (where one of the birth parents is African-

American) probably face the most prejudice, because black-white racial dynamics in the United States remain complex and politicized.

Ann and Tom E., a white couple who adopted two African-American siblings, ages one and two at the time of the interview, noted that although they had not—yet—experienced "out-and-out" prejudice as the result of their adoption decisions, they had faced a series of obnoxious reactions from assorted sources, including

- an African-American coworker who stopped speaking to Ann, citing the old NABSW line that transcultural adoption is "racial genocide";
- a cousin who asked Ann's mother how dark her children were;
- a coworker who wanted to know if the children were "crack babies";
- an aunt who asked in amazement, upon learning that the little girl was already highly verbal, "She speaks English?"; and, perhaps worst of all,
- a therapist who, upon evaluating Ann's son's development, made the comment: "Don't worry about him in school, he can always play sports."

"The assumption," Ann says, "is that if a child is African-American and a ward of the state, there must be something wrong with him or his biological family. Whether there is or isn't, it's no one's business."

Confronting Our Own Prejudice

Through our own use of ethnic jokes and stereotypes, we parents often unwittingly allow various forms of prejudice to become accepted within our lives. Yet, as adoptive parents who have made the leap into another culture—and who feel fiercely protective of our children—we have the added responsibility of being more sensitive to what prejudice is, including the ways that we may express it ourselves. We may observe prejudice in its more obvious and hateful forms, but it can also be subtle, and if we haven't experienced it ourselves, at least we can learn as much as possible about it for our children's sake, and for ours.

Many of us may not be "in touch" with our prejudicial attitudes. Perhaps we have a lot to think about as we express what we call "humor" when we *think* that what we are saying doesn't apply to us. A mother reports:

> My husband and I [both European-American] have three African-American children. Tonight, he shared a joke with a friend in front of me:
>
> "When does a Mexican become a Spaniard? When he marries your daughter."
>
> I caught my husband's eye and said very quietly, "And when does a nigger become an African-American?"
>
> He looked very sadly at me and replied, "Oh. That wasn't a very funny joke, was it?"
>
> He and I have talked about handling ethnic jokes—ANY ethnicity—but I don't think he thinks of responses at the crucial moment in a group, and, like tonight, he doesn't always think about the fact that it WAS an ethnic joke.

> Considering we are teaching our children—especially our about-to-be-kindergartner—about handling what other people say, I am a little concerned about this. As a stay-at-home mom (a.k.a. "doing full-time research on early childhood development"), I am often around folks who are ethnically sensitive/politically correct, but he is not.
>
> By the way, to his credit, a year or so ago my husband shared a story about a guy at work who was making some rather racist remarks. My husband enjoyed taking the opportunity to say, "Have you seen a picture of my kids?" when other family photos were being passed.

I asked Sue and Hector Badeau if they thought they had made any mistakes over the course of two decades of parenting in a multicultural family. "Lots," they laughed. But then Sue added, "When we embarked on adopting we figured that since we weren't racist, we were just the types of parents who could handle an interracial adoption."

What neither she nor Hector acknowledged at the time were some of the biases they harbored as the result of being white. One day, their son, José, who was born in El Salvador, came home from school and complained that someone had called him a nigger. "We dismissed it as that person's problem," says Sue. "The essence of our strategy was to tell José not to let this bother him. But by doing that, we were denying the reality of *his* experience."

Parents whose background is different from their child's, continues Sue—especially when the parents are white and the children are not—

> simply cannot say, "I know how you feel," because it hasn't happened to us. When we begin to understand what our children are going through—even if it's not part of our own experience—we allow them to have real feelings.

Nowadays, when Sue Badeau runs an introductory workshop on adoption, she always asks people to raise their hand if they're prejudiced. She usually finds that she's the first to put up her hand. Others then follow—and then the discussion starts.

It's never pleasant to acknowledge our own prejudice—stereotypes about certain racial or ethnic groups, for instance—but it's a healthy starting point, whether we're looking at current family dynamics or considering adoption for the first time. Cheri Register observes:

> One of the benefits of being an adoptive parent is how my own racial outlook has changed. I've always thought of myself as enlightened and liberal about race, but I never expected it to pervade my life and consciousness the way it has. But as the result of having my daughters, it has become a really important subject for me to explore—to look at "whiteness" as race and how much is taken for granted.

I do think we need to explore our own potential biases as we look at the type of family we wish to have and can accept. As we do so, we may also find that we can learn and change.

Our ability to change, however, requires a willingness to consider the impact of race in many of our children's lives, and from a young age. I was moved to think more deeply on this subject after reading the following observation by Gail

Steinberg, one of the directors of Pact, An Adoption Alliance, which is based in San Francisco. She reports:

> My four grown children—all adopted—range in age from twenty-nine to thirty-eight. They are Korean, African-American, Caucasian, and biracial. I could not be more proud of them nor of the strength of our family circle. The important thing they have taught me is how much race matters—not theories about race, but the reality that as people of color they have had significantly different experiences than I have had every day, even though we lived in the same family and interacted with the same community, institutions, and individuals.
>
> If I could go back and be a better parent, I would do as much as I could to prepare—not protect—them. I wish that when they were little I had had the wit and wisdom to be conscious of differences between their experiences and my white assumptions.
>
> I believe race is part of every conversation in our society, whether we notice it or not. From my experience, I believe that providing our kids with the tools and support to navigate through racial issues is as important to their healthy growth as clean air and fresh water.

In considering the type of adoption you will undertake, key considerations are what will work for you individually, what will work within the community where you live, with your family, and with other people who matter.

For example, Terry G., an international lawyer in New York City, decided to adopt a little girl from Vietnam because Terry herself had lived in Vietnam and spoke some Vietnamese. Living in lower Manhattan, she was close to Chinatown, which also has a significant Vietnamese community. Terry had a depth of understanding of Vietnamese culture that can only come from having firsthand experience.

I have participated in several on-line discussion groups in which people have debated the challenges of cross-cultural adoption. In some cases, white parents-to-be turn toward interracial adoption (seeking a black or biracial child) as a first choice: more than anything they want to be parents, and they know that they will be able to adopt more quickly this way than if they were to choose to wait for a white child. (In the U.S. foster care system, there are many more black children than white children awaiting permanent placement, and fewer black families available to adopt children.)

This was the case with Carol and Daniel K., who started to explore adoption when Carol did not become pregnant. "When our agency called and said the child was African-American, Daniel and I just looked at each other and said, 'Okay, that's fine. We want to be parents,' " she says. This decision did not meet with instant acceptance from family members, but the family's endorsement was not critical to the couple.

Prejudice from Family Members

Family members often try to influence our adoption decisions. If we're close to them and rely on them for emotional (and sometimes financial) support, their reactions may make a difference to us. Adoptive parents often discover that other folks—particularly family members—feel entitled to comment on our choices, when it's really none of their business. Some of our relatives who express discomfort with our choices may "come around" eventually, but not always. And then we face these options:

1. to continue to try to educate family members to understand what we're doing and why, and to seek their support, acceptance, and participation in family events;

2. to use gentle persuasion when an inappropriate incident occurs;

3. to make a "scene" if the incident is wildly out of line; or

4. to freeze out family members if they don't "come around."

A fifth choice is to continue to interact with problematic family members despite a high level of discomfort, and with the knowledge that the situation is unlikely to change. This scenario may become intolerable—and may lead to going with option 4.

Here are some situations that adoptive families have reported:

EXAMPLE I: JEALOUS STEPSISTER

I never expected that something like this would happen in my family, but it really bothered me when it did, so here goes: The other day, my much-older half sister (age sixty-eight), who has six children ranging in age from thirty to forty-two, paid my father (who is ninety-four) her semiannual visit. (Bear in mind that she lives less than five miles away from him.) They were driving somewhere in the car, and my dad started telling a cute story about something Olivia had done. My sister cut him off with, "Olivia this and Olivia that. I am sick of hearing about Olivia all the time. I have six children that are your REAL grandchildren and I never hear you say anything about them." Can you believe that? And to top it off, this woman is Olivia's godmother!

The grandfather's reply was right on target. According to Olivia's mother, he said:

"Olivia is my real grandchild too. I love all my grandchildren, but Olivia is special. She has brought a lot of happiness into my life." I never expected to encounter such an attitude in my family, but it makes me wish I had picked a different godmother for my daughter.

EXAMPLE 2: WHEN GRANDPARENTS ONLY SEE STEREOTYPES

The white mother of two African-American children reports:

We have a mixture of responses from family members to our children, Gary (almost three) and Lily (eighteen months). My mother started out by saying, "Those people always . . ." I was VERY angry about that because she was not seeing my son as a person. Mostly I just corrected her by saying, "Gary is . . ."

For this family, time and exposure were great teachers.

> After a year or so my mother was completely bowled over by Gary's magnetic personality, and [she] hasn't turned back. She is, in many ways, ignorant about lots of things, nervous about new things, and tries to generalize to make herself comfortable. This can be annoying, but it's unavoidable. This month she even complimented me on how cute Lily's hair looked. Lily's hair is very curly, but she is bald around the edges.

The paternal grandparents have also had to adjust their conception of family, Gary and Lily's mother writes, since her husband's brother and his wife also adopted two African-American children, a boy and a girl:

> At first [the paternal grandparents] weren't very comfortable but they seem to have adjusted.

EXAMPLE 3: SEPARATE AND UNEQUAL

The grandmother and aunt in a large extended family that includes biological and adopted children—many of them now young adults—have made a point of being particularly attentive to the biological children but not to the adopted children. The parents think they know why: several of the adopted children are African-American, and the relatives are not willing to acknowledge their racism toward these children.

Some of the adopted siblings live in the same New England town as the grandmother. "My mother traveled to Chicago to visit our biological daughter one summer but won't take the time to drive five minutes to see any of the others," the mother told me.

When the adopted children were still home with their parents, the grandparents reached out to all the grandchildren, and the grandfather was particularly involved. After he died, and as some of the children grew up and moved out on their own, the grandmother's attitude changed.

This situation has deeply hurt both the adopted children and their parents, who have tried, to no avail, to raise their concerns with the grandmother. They are considering cutting off contact as a last resort. This is not what they want to do, but the status quo is unacceptable. (The adoptive parents note that they have already cut off ties with the other pair of grandparents, who have never accepted their multiracial grandchildren.)

EXAMPLE 4: WHEN FAMILY MEMBERS DO COME AROUND

A mother writes:

> My father-in-law, who died after a nine-month battle with lung cancer, was always pretty racist. He and his wife discouraged us from adopting from China or anywhere. They didn't even come meet us at the airport or come over to see us for weeks after we brought home our new daughter, and they live only thirty miles away. However, since the first day they came over and he held Angelica, she became his favorite. He was always telling everyone how smart and pretty she was.
>
> During his illness, she could make him smile, and he was so proud of her. He told my husband that he was so glad we adopted her. He even requested memorials be made to children's foundations because that is what he thought really

> mattered. So those of you who have relatives or friends who are not encouraging, remember that people sometimes come around. Children have a way of doing that to even the toughest of them.
>
> Anyway, a husband and wife came to bring food, and when my mother-in-law introduced them to us she added, "and this is their daughter Angelica." The couple just kept looking at the baby. I finally added, "Angelica was born in China." They smiled at each other and said, "We thought so. Our granddaughter is from China." They showed us pictures. They were very proud! But it was really cool that in Durant, Oklahoma, of all places, we would run into these nice people. It goes to show you that you never know why people may be staring at our children. I think that is why I try to be more tolerant of people and not hateful.

Often the realities of family prejudice are not clear-cut. You may feel that your relatives accept you and your children on an equal basis with others, yet they remain ambivalent on race issues or continue to use inappropriate stereotypes. In these instances, patience and persistence are crucial.

Carol K. says that some of her closest relatives, who supported her adoptions, have sometimes let loose with clumsy racial stereotypes. When this happens, she intervenes immediately, but usually in a subtle and gentle way. Other times, though, she will be more aggressive. The goal is less to educate these people than to defend her family.

> When someone you believe in, who you know is opposed to racism, says something improper, pointing out their biases can

be effective. Other people simply have to be told outright not to say things. Even then, you won't necessarily change their attitudes in any way, but you and your family won't get subjected to comments unnecessarily.

It's a mistake for those of us who've adopted minority children ever to allow our children, and ourselves, to be subjected to inappropriate comments from people who aren't interested in changing, no matter how close we are to them, or how embarrassing it is [to have to say something to these people]. We were worried (but committed to the fact) that we might have to keep our children away from certain members of my husband's family. It hasn't worked out that way, but if they hadn't behaved, we would have left.

Prejudice in Your Community

If you don't think that the community you live in—and by "community" I mean not just your actual neighborhood, but also the schools, workplace, house of worship, and other institutions that may be important to you—will be accepting of the family you intend to create, then perhaps you need to consider making a change. This change can be as drastic as moving, or as manageable as finding a different place to worship, talking to an institutional leader (such as a minister or the head of a particular organization) about a problem you perceive, becoming proactive (in a civic organization, for instance, by forming a committee or becoming an officer), or arranging private discussions with individuals whose words or actions may have sparked discomfort.

With regret, one parent reports:

> We have dropped lots of friends and acquaintances due to ignorant comments, jokes, and questions. One woman at church was trying to convince me that Gary was from India since his hair is on the straight side! Another told us a horrible joke with racial slurs a few months before we had Gary, and I remember thinking, "What will she say if our child is black?"

As was mentioned in Chapter 4, the perennial "family tree" assignments many children do in school may make adopted children feel uncomfortable and alienated. Your role is to suggest an alternative equitable approach to the work that does not stigmatize an adopted child. You'll probably be happily surprised at how a teacher accepts resources you might suggest—unless the teacher is so insecure and defensive that he or she won't consider other options. Try providing materials on alternatives to the family tree, or offer to run a workshop on adoption, diversity, and different views on how families are formed.

All of this work takes time, but you are investing in peace of mind. In some cases you may find that you misinterpreted certain actions or that a positively framed dialogue will lead to the change you seek. I would advise that you listen to some comments by older adoptees who look back on their childhood and wish they could have been raised in communities where there were more children like them. (The New York State Citizens' Coalition for Children has an archive of articles and speeches by older adoptees. See Chapter 8, Goods and Services.)

Prejudice in Schools

As parents, we need to be vigilant that our children are treated as individuals at school. As adoptive parents in cross-cultural families, we often need to take extra steps to ensure that teachers, principals, and other school professionals (and paraprofessionals) do not take our children for granted.

EXAMPLE 1: WHEN THE OFFENDER IS A TEACHER

A somewhat common experience is that schoolteachers, often inadvertently, allow a prejudicial incident to take place without addressing the dynamics that contributed to it. Parents are then faced with deciding how to handle the situation: do we let it go, do we communicate directly with the "perpetrator," or do we confront the school leadership?

The mother of two children, a son born to her and a daughter adopted from China, told of a situation involving her fourth-grade son. One day he came home from school and reported that he had lost recess time for talking during a lesson.

> He said he got in trouble for doing the right thing. A girl in back of him was poking fun at Chinese people (not particularly his sister). My son took offense and said that she was insulting his sister and asked her to stop. My child was singled out because he reacted. The teacher, not knowing the situation, punished him for talking during a lesson.

The boy's mother went to school to discuss what had happened and to complain that the penalty—serious for a fourth grader—was unfair.

> The teacher agreed, but when I told her [the name of the little girl] who was making fun of others, she said, "Oh, no, that doesn't sound like her. I can't believe she would do that."

Reflecting on this incident later, the mother realized that she still felt anger toward the teacher.

> I felt she had no right to make the judgment call that this girl would not do something like that, and therefore it seems to follow that my son is making it up. I will speak further to her on this matter at upcoming conferences.

EXAMPLE 2: WHEN THE OFFENDER IS SUPPORT STAFF

Other scenarios can be trickier. What do you do when you see a form of prejudice expressed by an assistant teacher or a nonprofessional staff member at school or day care? An assistant at Donna S.'s Chinese-born daughter's day-care center referred to her daughter Ellen as "China." The assistant was African-American. Donna remembers:

> I was beside myself. I equated this young girl calling Ellen "China" with my calling [the assistant] "Africa" or a Hispanic person "Mexico." I felt something should be said. I didn't think the assistant meant any harm, but I found it very insensitive, and didn't want this type of insensitivity, inadvertent or not, perpetuated.

Donna contacted the day-care center director about the incident, eliciting a promise to talk to the assistant. She also requested a follow-up meeting with the director and the assistant, which took place the next day.

> The assistant claimed she had used the expression "China" because she couldn't remember Ellen's name, but she said she hadn't meant any harm. I calmly told her that to use that term was insensitive and derogatory. She looked at me like I was from Mars. I told her it was the same as if I'd used the *n*-word or called her by the country of her ancestry.
>
> She still didn't get it. "Well," she told me, "you know, she has 'Chinky' eyes and looks like a little China doll, so I called her China." I was even more shocked! She promised not to say it again and went back to work. The director, meanwhile, talked about how diverse this day-care center was—even though she conceded that Ellen was the only Asian child. I asked the director to plan a staff meeting to discuss issues of diversity and sensitivity.

Nothing happened, so Donna and her husband then arranged to meet the regional director of the day-care center (which is part of a network of day-care centers). The upshot of that meeting was an agreement to hold a mandatory staff diversity training workshop, to arrange for the center director (who had been on the job for just six months) to be "mentored" by another director who was more experienced in diversity issues, to communicate the situation to a parents' committee, and to put a letter regarding this episode in the assistant's personnel file. Donna sums up her feelings about the situation:

> We considered—for a second—removing Ellen from this day care after the incident. But the bottom line is that she has thrived here, and other than with the new person, the care has been excellent. Unfortunately, we may all face this type of is-

sue in the future, and we need to be as prepared as possible, remain calm, and help our children be aware of some of these issues. We also have to learn always to keep an open line of communication between both sides. We can educate only one narrow mind at a time.

EXAMPLE 3: WHEN THE OFFENDER IS A CHILD

Sometimes young children unwittingly reflect stereotypes they either learned from family members or picked up from other sources (cartoons, for instance). In an on-line discussion, a mother of a girl adopted from China wrote:

> Two of my son's good friends made up a really yucky song starting something like "Me Chinese, me no sneeze, me . . ." (whatever, whatever . . . I don't know the words, but it is bad). I am having one of the mothers over for coffee next week and feel comfortable mentioning this incident to her. She will be appalled, I am sure.

The mother of the adopted Chinese girl wanted suggestions on how to deal with this type of experience—both how to talk to other parents and how to broach the problem at her children's school. One idea was to volunteer to read a story about tolerance and acceptance geared toward her daughter's age group. The mother responded:

> But my problem is that it is not just isolated to the classroom. I know the kids who are doing this, and they are good kids, but I don't think they understand their actions.

Having resources (see Part IV, Resources) can be a big help. So can constant exposure to multicultural images in our daily lives, including the books and magazines that we read to our children, and the videos and other materials we have at home, as well as outside activities that help develop an awareness of a "larger" world. In addition, adults supervising children's play should be vigilant for instances of inappropriate behavior and use them as learning experiences.

Anti-Adoption Prejudice

There are times when people, wittingly or unwittingly, express an opinion about adoption that reflects a sense that this approach to forming a family is somehow second-best to having biological children.

The following episode touches on all types of adoption:

> I just got home from dropping my daughter off at her nursery school. We were the first ones there, so the teacher, my daughter, and I were sitting together on those little chairs, chatting, when the assistant teacher walked in and proceeded to say, "Hi, you guys, sorry if I'm late. My daughter was so BAD this morning, she was just impossible . . . . Would you like to adopt her?"
>
> My mouth dropped open. Now I'm trying to decide whether I should say something to that teacher with my daughter there, after class (did my daughter Lia even notice this incident? If so, has she forgotten it?—she's two and a half), or say something to the teacher privately, or complain about [the assistant] to the principal, or what.
>
> I know it probably would have been best to speak up right

then, but darn it, my sluggish morning brain just didn't process the situation that fast!

A day later, after she'd regained her composure, the mother communicated her feelings to the head teacher, who then spoke privately to the assistant teacher. The assistant teacher was very embarrassed—even hurt—to know that she had made such an inadvertent gaffe. But, rest assured, she will never do that again!

As parents, we may wish to discuss some of these issues with caregivers and teachers in advance in order to head off such a careless, thoughtless mistake.

Some Thoughts on Coping with Prejudice

1. *Always think of your child first!* If your child is with you, make sure that whatever response you make is geared toward what your child will hear. Thus formulate a constructive response (no matter how much you may be boiling over inside) rather than one that may be blistering and critical. If someone should say to you, "Why did you adopt a [child of a different background or a child from a different country] instead of a child similar to yourself?" put your arms around your child and say, "Why not?"

   You also need to consider the source and tone of the other person's remark. If this person is a friend or someone investigating adoption, the question may be an earnest inquiry about making choices. Another popular reply is: "Because that's where my son/daughter was."

2. *Is it really prejudice—or just ignorance?* Sometimes it's hard to tell the difference. If you're not sure, figure out a gentle, and perhaps even generous, response that may serve to inform and enlighten the other person. If someone should make a blatant statement about the nature of your child's background, a good comeback is, "Where did you get your information? I did a lot of research before I adopted, and that's not what *I* found out." (I was taken aback when a man in my synagogue asserted that my daughter "could never be a real Jew because she was born a Buddhist." How did *he* know?)

   Sometimes, though, the statements people make are so surprising and unexpected that it's hard to find words to reply. A father of a child my daughter's age once said to me on a playground, "Oh, the Chinese get rid of all their rejects, don't they?" Although this statement may have reflected ignorance about the situation in China rather than downright prejudice, I was too shocked and angry at his tactlessness to say anything. I took my daughter's hand and left. Sadie was too young at the time to understand this statement. I think that a wise response would have been—again, for Sadie's benefit—"She's the daughter I always wanted. Good-bye." If she were not in earshot, I might have explained the circumstances that lead to Chinese infant girls being placed for adoption, and pointed out that many of these wonderful, beloved girls are ultimately adopted (in China as well as elsewhere) because of a policy designed to find good homes for them.

3. *And when what is said is very objectionable . . . then what?* If someone who has been a friend says something truly objectionable—again, think of your child first, not the friend. The "friend" may not be worth keeping. I have had some so-called friends criticize my decision to adopt from China for a range of reasons: Why go overseas when there are so many needy children in the United States? (There are needy children around the world. This is how I chose to adopt. And, by the way, it's none of your business.) Why didn't you just try to have a baby of "your own"? (She *is* my own.) And so on.

Some of the most unpleasant experiences may involve other individuals of the same racial or ethnic background as your child. As I mentioned earlier, the white mother of an African-American child was ostracized by an African-American coworker because of her adoption choice. In my own case, one of the worst encounters I have had was with an ethnically Chinese woman from Malaysia who demanded to know how much I had "paid" for my daughter. To me, this statement constituted not just ignorance but a form of prejudice, because it commodified my daughter individually and us as a family, rather than acknowledging adoption as a way to form a family. I said, simply, "I adopted her because I wanted a family." The woman insisted that babies were sold in China and asked, again, how much I had paid. I had been about to purchase a toy this woman was selling. I put the toy down, took my money back, and walked away. I sometimes pass her store—with Sadie—and walk by

> brusquely. I doubt she remembers this episode, but I'll never forget it.

I know of many adoptive parents of African-American children who have been thrilled with how their own children are welcomed, especially if the parents reach out to the African-American community for support. Similarly, when I think about the many positive encounters I have had with Chinese and Chinese-American people, including complete strangers, I know that the storekeeper's attitudes by no means reflect how Chinese people in general perceive adopted Chinese children.

A Final Reflection

During the time I was writing this book, an episode of exceptional violence took place in Los Angeles: a white gunman, later revealed to be a member of a hate group, shot at children attending a Jewish-run day camp. A Jewish woman living in Los Angeles with her little girl adopted from China wrestled with how to deal with this incident.

> We know two kids who attend camp there, but thankfully, they were not at camp that day. When the shootings happened, my daughter's day camp brought all the kids inside and locked the doors. They explained to the kids what was happening, so my daughter, who is six and a half, knows all the details. Yesterday, she came home from camp and informed me that the "bad guy" had been caught.
>
> The only thing she doesn't know is the "why." I am wondering whether I should tell her. I don't want her to walk

> around thinking that someone may shoot her because she is Jewish. On the other hand, at some point, she needs to know about anti-Semitism. Also complicating matters is that she is Chinese, so the chances of her personally experiencing anti-Semitism are not that high. She is more likely to have problems because she is Chinese.

This is just the sort of challenge many parents may face. Probably the wisest approach is to inform our children that a few troubled people behave in inappropriate ways, but that there are various positive ways that we may respond. (Organizations such as the Anti-Defamation League and the Southern Poverty Law Center's Teaching Tolerance Program, listed in Part IV, Resources, have developed educational materials to address such issues.) It would be nice to imagine that there will be a time when we will not have to face such questions. But for the time being, confronting and communicating these issues in age-appropriate ways is probably a far better solution than pretending these uncomfortable problems don't exist.

six

As Our Kids Grow Older

■

Letting Them Take the Lead

A friend of mine is having a lot of difficulty with her sixteen-year-old son, who was adopted as an infant from Korea. He's doing a lot of acting out, doing poorly in school, and so forth, and generally causing his mother to tear her hair out. Often he points out to her that because she isn't Asian, she can't understand his life and what's going on with him. The other day, he expanded on that theme with this [paraphrased] exchange:

Kid: You just don't understand. Asian teenagers are different.

Mom: Explain to me how they're different.

Kid: Well, we're just focused on different things than white kids. For instance, when Asian boys get together, all we talk about is girls and cars.

Mom (trying desperately not to laugh): And you don't think white teenage boys talk about girls and cars?

Kid: No, they think about other things.

Needless to say, my friend was flabbergasted by this, but she has decided that it's just proof that even teenagers don't understand transracial issues most of the time.

I've mentioned this anecdote to a number of parents of adopted kids. A few chuckle in recognition. But most acknowledge that being adopted probably *does* have something to do with what the boy is going through, and that the mother should not have been so dismissive. By talking about feeling different, this son was possibly inviting his mother to have a serious talk. Indeed, one of the lessons of such an episode is that the young man may well have been sending a message between the lines that his mother did not get—perhaps by choice. We should not let that happen.

Growing Pains

We need to bear in mind a few core issues facing our children as they grow older.

1. They will have a greater awareness that they're different.

2. They have an essential desire NOT to be different.

3. Some of our kids may express a greater need than others to know more about "where I came from," including a deeper understanding of what led to their being available for adoption.

4. Some may not want to know where they came from—or they will prefer to internalize it.

While we should begin telling them their story at the earliest age possible, their ability to absorb what actually happened to them—including the magnitude of the loss of their biological connection—evolves as they grow older. Some children may, indeed, enter a grieving phase long after you had thought they were at peace with their situation. For some, this grieving may constitute a genuine depression. Be alert to such a possibility, and, as always, "be there."

Lois Ruskai Melina's *Making Sense of Adoption* is full of suggested conversations and activities parents might want to read up on in case they encounter (or anticipate) a conflict related to adolescent angst. Our older children may be less than open with us. Not only is it the adolescent "way" to be less communicative, but adoptees who are struggling with their unique identity issues—and perhaps groping for ties to their birth roots—may hold back because they may fear hurting their adoptive parents. (Melina also publishes a fine on-line newsletter on raising adopted children.)

One of our responsibilities will be to train ourselves to become excellent listeners—to acknowledge the authenticity of our children's feelings (and be grateful when they express them). We must also, in a way, become "co-conspirators" (sometimes actively, other times without their knowing), to work on a strategy to help them come to terms with critical identity issues, especially during adolescence, so that they can emerge with their integrity and self-esteem intact. At a certain point, they may gravitate to peers rather than to us to deal with these issues. But it doesn't mean we should withdraw. They still need us!

Grappling with Adoption and Identity Issues

THE ADOPTION ISSUE

Some thoughtful writers have articulated excellent strategies for addressing the push-pull of the adoption identity dilemma. Most of these involve role-playing in various scenarios that we may anticipate at different phases of our children's lives. These strategies may be particularly useful as our kids get older and may feel less inclined to talk about what's bothering them.

A wonderful book for younger children is *Talking with Young Children About Adoption* by Mary Watkins and Susan Fisher. It outlines the milestones of children's perceptions about adoption from toddlerhood onward and helps parents understand how our children perceive being different, not just because they were adopted but because they *look* different. The book then provides a framework for parents to begin to tell the adoption story in the most basic way.

Sometimes telling the story on our own is awkward. We don't know how. Some of us may be waiting for our children to bring up the topic, and, for one reason or another, they may not, so the role-playing scenarios we read up on in order to prepare ourselves for this important discussion just don't work. In those cases, storybooks such as *Over the Moon* by Karen Katz; *An Mei's Strange and Wondrous Journey* by Stephen Molnar-Fenton; and *Mommy Far, Mommy Near* by Carol Peacock are excellent. Each thoughtfully tells a little girl's adoption story from her parents' or her own point of view. The girl tells of her fantasies of her birth family as well as her experiences of looking different from her adoptive family. *Over the Moon* is simple enough to be understood and loved by a three-year-old, and the drawings are colorful and joyful. *An Mei's Journey*, "told" by six-year-old An Mei with dreamy illustrations, is closer to magical realism, as An Mei tries to imagine all the circumstances that led to her being adopted. *Mommy Far, Mommy Near* is more delicate and more appropriate, since it touches directly on the hurt or loss that a child feels because she looks different from her adoptive parents, and because she knows that somewhere there is a family in China that she once belonged to. The story ends on a very affirming note, however.

Parents can use these books in different ways and at different times as our children grow up and come to understand more "layers" of the stories in the books—and more layers in their own story. (The books mentioned here are described in more detail in Chapter 7.)

If our children are struggling with being adopted, it does not matter, for instance, if we say, "Well, think of Joelle, Rachel, and Louise. They're also adopted from Peru and don't look just like their parents. But you see them all the time, and they're doing fine." Do we really know that? When the situation revolves around a cultural issue related to the specific nature of adoption—the issue of abandonment is a key concern in Chinese adoptions—no amount of reassurance can erase this reality. As one mother told me, "Jenny doesn't care about all the other girls from China whom we know. She's worried about HER abandonment story, and the birth mom she'll never know."

The writer Cheri Register observes, "The loss of the birth mother can be so painful to girls and adolescents. Puberty can be an explosive time anyway, and the loss of the birth-mother bond can be especially critical for some."

Register notes that she has seen this problem more frequently with girls than boys. Her own daughter was treated for depression at age fifteen, and although the immediate cause was a troubled relationship with a boy, she was able, through therapy, to acknowledge an underlying fear of abandonment, exacerbated by Register's divorce when her girls were quite young.

But not just therapy helped—so did growing up. By the time I chatted with Register, one daughter was in college and the other was about to finish high school. Register says: "A lot of my worries have been put to rest because of the way my family has grown. My daughters and I are close, and they seem to have come to terms with some of the conflicts of their teens. Yes, many of the things I thought through heavily in the beginning and agonized about later have turned out to be serious issues, but not 'troubling.' And some were easier to deal with than I thought."

If Register's comments give the impression that "things will work out," bear in mind that she has been in the forefront of adoption thinking and writing for many years. She also experienced single cross-cultural motherhood before it was as common as it is now. Her overriding message, as I have said, is the need to be vigilant and to communicate from the time your children are little.

HELPING OUR CHILDREN COPE WITH BEING DIFFERENT

As our children get older, they will evolve into a new level of consciousness about what it means to be adopted and to be different. As they reach the typical developmental milestones, they will increasingly seek to find out who they "are."

Parents I've spoken with report that as early as age four, their children start to express concerns about being different from family members and friends, and not belonging in the environment in which they live, if they don't see many of their counterparts or many potential role models. Children's awareness of difference can create real distress as they get older—especially when other children point out their differentness—and can leave them feeling confused, sad, and sometimes angry. The degree to which children can show, and share, their feelings may vary depending on their personality, their relationship to you, the opportunities they have in their environment to see (and befriend) people who are similar to them, and other variables. The source of these feelings can be multifaceted. No amount of ethnic food, videotapes, or culture classes can allay the internal anxiety.

Real Parents, Real Children, by Holly van Gulden and Lisa M. Bartels-Rabb, is particularly helpful in addressing the issues related to adopted adolescents. As teens, our children will become acutely aware of racial difference and may be subjected to intense peer pressure to "declare" their race. I would speculate that this pressure may subside somewhat as the number of mixed-race families increases and an awareness of being biracial increases. Just the same, teenagers sometimes face situations that may seem irrational to parents but can be magnified among children whose background is clearly mixed or whose parents look different. Anticipating such occurrences is important for parents—and this is another reason that parents may want to find a living and educational environment that offers our children a comfort zone where they do not feel like outsiders because they are with other children like them.

Some years ago I attended an adoption seminar that featured a panel of young adult adoptees discussing their experiences growing up. A young woman, now in college, described what happened when a boy in her high school class—they were both seniors—brought her to his home to meet his parents. The family was Jewish, and the parents were intent on ensuring that their son dated only Jewish girls. This girl had darker skin than the young man, reflecting her *mestiza*—mixed Latina and Indian—ethnicity.

She *was* born in Latin America and probably did have some "indigenous" blood. She was also Jewish—like her parents here in the United States. The boy subsequently told this young girl that they couldn't go out anymore. His parents had objected.

How did she react? seminar participants asked. Well, she shrugged, if that was how he felt, she didn't need him. This was a woman who appeared to be secure in her sense of self and was able to let go of an unpleasant situation. At least in this setting she didn't sound bitter.

The type of networking we do with our children when they are young—joining support groups and attending culture camps, for instance—can have a real payoff when they get older. These institutions reinforce a positive sense of identity and assure adopted children that they are not alone. Cheri Register notes that many of her daughters' friends were also adopted, and that the Twin Cities area, where they live, has a long tradition of cross-cultural adoption, especially from Korea. As teens, her girls will want to fit in as much as possible with their peer group—*assimilation* is often the key word here—and "assimilating" with other adoptees in a peer group is a way to feel secure.

An adoptive mother who is involved in Jewish communal activities mentioned that her Mexican-American daughter had become self-conscious because she was darker-skinned than the other children in her Hebrew school. Being part of a network of multiracial Jewish families made a huge difference to this girl, because when these families get together, no child stands out. "Eight-year-olds are very concrete in their observations," says the mother, who is a social worker. "So Robin is aware that she is darker-skinned than most Jews she meets. But now she says that you can't always tell who's Jewish by looking at them." The family also belongs to a synagogue known for having an unusually large multiracial membership. At the time they joined, the synagogue president was black.

When I chatted with Robin myself, she was somewhat dismissive of the racial issues. But I would speculate that this is because her mother has been aggressive in seeking opportunities for Robin to meet other children like her. In addition, Robin has another set of priorities to deal with: she has learning disabilities to overcome in order to succeed in primary school and Hebrew school.

Sometimes we may see our older children taking on different personalities—one with us, one with different sets of friends. This quality may seem particularly marked in interracial adoptees, who may feel pressure to "behave" in different ways with different peer groups. The Jewish father of an African-American teenager who had attended a Jewish day school and could speak Hebrew joked that his son spoke "Hebonics," a type of teenage slang that mixed the urban "street" lingo of African-American youth with the influence of his school.

Teens who have been adopted internationally will tend to identify with second-generation children of their own or a similar ethnic background because these children may confront similar challenges. For instance, second-generation Asian-Americans and Asian adoptees often face a common assumption that they don't speak English and aren't American citizens. For adoptees, the "perception experience" is magnified by the fact that their parents don't resemble them (unless, of course, the children were adopted by Asians), and often they have a surname that does not "match" their looks.

Adopted children who "look" different may blend in well with their peers, have friends, go dating, just like other children. And a number of studies (cited in the books mentioned above) have shown that our children generally do fine in the self-esteem category, as long as we are conscientious in reinforcing the wholeness of their identity. Mary Watkins and Susan Fisher note that transracially adopted children may even outperform their same-race peers because of economic advantage: they tend to be adopted by middle- and upper-middle-class families. But being different may place them in a potentially awkward situation to which we should be alert. The situation can be especially delicate during the teen years.

One mother writes:

> My two daughters are now young women of color, and we have had many lengthy conversations regarding the attention they received throughout the years. Both have suffered from always being on "display." Neither sees it as positive, only as

> an affirmation of how different they are. They don't believe it is their "beauty" that attracts people, but their color. Ever since they came to us, they have been told by total strangers just how beautiful, gorgeous, exotic, they are . . . how we will need to get a bat to keep the boys away, how we'd better watch out or someone might just run off with one of those girls (highlighted by laughter and a playful manner). People have gone out of their way, across crowded rooms, to make a big deal of their eyes, hair, and skin tones. Since we adopted them we have never been able to go anywhere without stares (good and bad) or comments (primarily positive).
>
> I realized when we adopted our daughters that we were choosing to be "different," that we would attract attention because we were not a traditional family. I expected the stares and comments, and at first I felt they would only reflect positively on our children. It is such a self-esteem boost to have someone talk so well of them.
>
> However, I was not aware how hard they would take it as they grew up. They rarely make eye contact with others, so that they can pretend they don't know they are being stared at. They avoid "stranger conversations." They want to blend in, but they cannot do that if they are with us. They want to go to a restaurant and not have people comment. To have one's appearance constantly pointed out has not been good for our girls.

Indeed, this parent notes, the daughters' appearance of "ignoring" everything around them gives people the impression that they are

> aloof, stuck-up, and less social. This is not the case at all, and once someone becomes part of their inner circle, they often

> comment on how caring, sweet, fun, and friendly the girls are. Apparently their need to feel autonomous leads to body language that appears less than friendly. It's a survival skill at best, but one that has harmed them emotionally.

Striking out on their own, the girls—now young women—have asserted the identity they are most comfortable with. The older daughter, in college, shares a dorm room with her best friend, who is African-American. Her friendships have been very diverse, but mainly with people of color. Some confusion remains, though, and the mother reports:

> She says she still feels "funny," because she does not really "fit" into any one world and continues to have that sense that people are looking at her, and want their questions answered. Thankfully she is willing to share her feelings with us, and we can speak openly.

Certainly, the openness this parent describes is key.

As our children get older, they may choose to focus on learning more about their birth identity, and they may not want to participate in some aspects of family life. For instance, in a discussion group involving Jewish adoptive families, the mother of an adopted Korean-born teenager described her son's behavior:

> My oldest (son) didn't really consider being Korean very important until he was in eighth grade. Then it became VERY important, and identity issues have taken the forefront. For several years, he has associated *only* with Asian kids. Only Asian things mattered; he didn't consider Judaism part of his

> life (and still doesn't). This hasn't really happened yet with my daughter, but she is so involved with athletics (soccer, basketball, softball, track, volleyball) that she hasn't had much space to consider it.

Adolescence is a time of great identity exploration—and a time when religious observance often becomes an imposition for children. Should we create a family furor when our children resist our requests to become more involved? Or should we support them even if their decisions seem, on the surface, to pull us apart? Or should we try, somehow, to find a middle ground?

Joy Kim Lieberthal, who was adopted from Korea at age six in 1975 and is now a social worker specializing in adoption, said: "The most important things to me are the essential parenting issues: do what's best for your child, but remember, she is *your* child, even if she was born to another mother." Her point is that whatever cultural activities and influences we may wish to pursue on our children's behalf, our first obligation is to nurture our children. Joy's family sent their several Korean daughters to Korean school, and Joy hated it. "You shouldn't push that," she told me. "I often loved learning about my mother's Irish culture. That's one of the great things about being in a multiethnic family."

Sometimes children may become more anxious if, for instance, they are the only adopted child in a family that includes biological children, or if the biological family looks distinctly different from the adopted child.

Kyle Messner is a professor of multicultural education, has a daughter adopted from China, and has a brother, Kim, who was adopted from Korea as a little boy but who is now an adult. In the on-line magazine *FamilyCulture.com* (January 2000), Kyle writes:

> When I was considering adopting my daughter from China, I asked Kim what his experience was growing up. He told me of times when kids called him "chink" in school. He also told me how he dreaded Pearl Harbor Day because he was afraid people would think he was Japanese and blame him. I asked him why he had never said anything, and he said, "Why should I have bothered you with it? What could you have done?" My brother shouldered the downside of being different on his own.

In a paper on transracial adoption prepared for the National Adoption Information Clearinghouse, author and social worker Debra W. Smith wrote that families may want to consider adopting more than one child (especially if there's a sibling group) in order to avoid the type of isolation Kim was only able to reveal to his sister when they were both adults. Of course, not all parents can—or want to—undertake more than one adoption.

As of yet I have not observed Sadie encountering these problems, but only now is she beginning to express an awareness of being different from other children, including not looking like me and having "another mother" in China. She will point out someone who looks Chinese and then say to me, "You're not Chinese." (She has recently grasped that some people who look Chinese come from Korea, so she is starting to realize that not everyone who "looks" like her is Chinese.)

Our Children Take the Lead

In the 1960s and 1970s, the opportunity to develop a sense of ethnic identity just didn't exist for the many Korean children who were placed with families throughout the United States. There were so few other cross-cultural adoptions then that the question of how the adoptees' identity issues were being handled did not come to the fore.

Many of these children grew up as the only Asian, or the only biracial, adoptee, or one of very few, in mainly white communities. Sometimes the only other people like them were their adopted siblings. A few culture camps did exist, but they were not nearly as sophisticated as the programs that are available today. Hollee McGinnis recalls that the best thing about the camps was seeing other children like her.

Joy Kim Lieberthal, also adopted from Korea, remembers the camp experience similarly. "It was really cool—all the counselors, all of us, we were the same. Everyone was adopted! There were no racial slurs, no teasing, and lots of positive feedback!"

The 1997 launch of Also-Known-As was a natural next step as Korean adoptees became adults. Other adoptee groups are organizing similar get-togethers as they reach adulthood in a critical mass. Hundreds of Vietnamese-born young adults, brought to the United States during the Vietnamese "baby-lift" of the mid-1970s, met in Baltimore in April 2000 to examine their own experiences growing up adopted in the United States in the context of the Vietnam War. As with some of the Korean adoptees, some of the Vietnamese babies were also of mixed ethnicity because their fathers were American or European military personnel.

As mentioned in Chapter 1, the magazine *Mavin* represents a further assertion of what it means to be "cross-cultural" by the young people whose unique experience this is. Each issue lists activities of organizations of mixed-race students on college campuses across the United States. The Fall 1999 issue (no. 3) focused on the transracial adoption experience. It featured an interview with Olympic champion Dan O'Brien, a biracial adoptee who grew up in a family where most of his siblings were also adopted and were of various racial and ethnic backgrounds, as well as profiles of a range of adoptive families. Cleverly, *Mavin* also inserts an adoption timeline into the feature, chronicling how transracial adoption patterns have evolved from 1946 to the present.

The very existence of *Mavin* underscores what a different world we live in. As culture globalizes, the gulfs that used to separate people from different backgrounds in different parts of the world are gradually being replaced by bridges. I can only begin to fathom what China will look like in ten or fifteen years, when my daughter and I might travel there together.

The change is already under way. Cheri Register says that when she and her daughters traveled to Korea in 1997, on a homeland tour under the auspices of the adoption agency she had used, she was concerned about how her girls would be received in what she felt was a conservative country. (She knew that she should avoid mentioning her divorce.) One daughter, Grace, had decided that she would keep her nose stud in and dress the "artsy" way she always dresses—in Indian gauze blouses and colorful skirts. They were waiting to meet the foster family who had taken care of Grace for the first ten months of her life. When the foster family's daughter came to pick them up, she was wearing a bright green Spandex pants outfit and heavy makeup. Grace fit in just fine and the whole family experienced a warm reunion. It was a critical moment for Grace, of course—to be accepted for who she was, without artifice.

Giving Our Children Some Space

Parents may feel threatened when their children assert their "difference" in a forceful way. But the children are establishing themselves as autonomous adults, just as we once did when we were their age. It is essential to bear in mind that throughout this process, adoptees are in no way denigrating adoption! The charter of Also-Known-As describes transracial adoption as

> a positive institution. Adoption is a clear expression *that although blood may be thicker than water, love is thicker than blood.* A person's choice to look past these differences shows that we have the ability to relate to others first as human beings. We support intercountry, interracial adoption because it works.

We parents play an essential role by supporting our growing children in their quest for identity, *listening* to them and acknowledging the validity of their feelings and desires. As many adoptees I spoke with have also said, we parents play an important role by making our children's birth culture available through activities, meals, holidays, reading materials, personal contacts, and other resources that will help our children understand their roots from the time they are very young.

But the search for roots, the journey "home," is, ultimately, theirs to take—or not. It is very tempting for well-meaning parents to initiate this journey, or to offer to go along with our children, and even to help locate the biological parents. But this is not *our* issue—it belongs to our children. As I mentioned earlier, some Korean adoptees have recommended that children should wait until they're in their twenties to go. I would have thought that was too long to wait—but, again, it's not *my* trip.

"I went at age twenty-four," Joy Kim Lieberthal told me. "And that's where I learned everything I now know about Korea. This trip is *nothing* like you'll ever do—and I don't advocate going alone! You expect things to be a certain way, and they're not." When she arrived at the airport, she recalls, it was the first time in her life that she was just another Asian woman with dark black hair—she was like everyone there!

And yet, says Joy now, "I love the fact that my family the Lieberthals [which includes four daughters adopted from Korea and two adopted from Vietnam] doesn't look the way people expect. Growing up as I did has been a really great way to learn tolerance and to cope in the world."

part iv

resources

seven

Publications

Whole books have been written to provide resource information on multicultural themes. Here is an eclectic guide to resources I consider the best for our families. Since new materials are constantly being produced, this list will exclude some that you may have found more recently. If that's the case, please contact me through the publisher for a possible update.

I have divided this section into several categories:

1. Catalogs and Information Resources
   - General Topics
   - Specializing in Ethnic Materials and/or Adoption
2. Miscellaneous Resources and Series
3. Magazines and Newsletters
4. Books and Book Series
   - Anthologies, Bibliographies, and Sourcebooks
   - Books for Adults
     - Ethnic Identity
     - Parenting
   - Books for Children
   - Multicultural Activities and Celebrations
     - Multicultural Activity Books
     - Celebrations
   - Book Series

1. *Catalogs and Information Resources*

GENERAL TOPICS

Anti-Defamation League
823 United Nations Plaza
New York, NY 10017
Phone: (800) 343-5540
Web site: *www.adl.org*

The ADL's catalog of "Resources for the Classroom and Community" offers a range of materials that look at multicultural issues, diversity, and anti-bias issues. "A World of Difference" is its multimedia diversity program, which includes videos, books, and lesson plans for teachers.

National Adoption Information Clearinghouse
33 C Street, SW
Washington, DC 20447
Phone: (703) 352-3488 or (888) 251-0075
Fax: (703) 385-3206
E-mail: *naic@calib.com*
Web site: *www.calib.com/naic/index.htm*

Established in 1987 as a service of the Children's Bureau within the Department of Health and Human Services, NAIC is not a catalog per se, but it offers outstanding information resources on almost every adoption issue, including current statistics and excellent articles on past and current trends in adoptions of all types. Much of the information is free, although there is a charge for some publications. (See also Country-Specific and Ethnic Adoption Web Sites and Listservs in Chapter 8, Goods and Services.)

Teaching Tolerance
Southern Poverty Law Center
400 Washington Avenue
Montgomery, AL 36101-0548
Phone: (334) 264-0286
Fax: (334) 264-3121
Web site: *www.splcenter.org*

Teaching Tolerance is the name of a media education program sponsored by the Southern Poverty Law Center to counter bigotry and hate crimes and promote tolerance across races, religions, and ethnicities. The program includes free materials (videos, texts, "One World" posters) and offers mini-grants to teachers, as well as magazines and other material for individual subscribers.

SPECIALIZING IN ETHNIC MATERIALS AND/OR ADOPTION

Weber State College
Clearinghouse for Multicultural/Bilingual Education
Web site: *www.Weber.edu/MBE/htmls/BME-Books*

Based at Weber State College in Minnesota, this Web site provides mounds of information listing publishers of reading materials, audiovisuals, and videos on multicultural topics.

It is updated regularly. The categories are wide-ranging, including Hispanic, African-American, Muslim, Asian, Native American, and many others.

Asia for Kids
Phone: (800) 765-5885 or (800) 888-9681
Fax: (800) 765-5889 or (513) 563-3105
E-mail: *info@afk.com*
Web site: *www.asiaforkids.com*

This is one of my favorite catalogs. Selina Yoon, a Korean skater, came to the United States and founded the catalog when her athletic career ended. Despite the name of the organization, you can find books, videos, and other materials that cross many different cultural areas and span many areas of the world, including Africa and Latin America. The range of materials is wide: books, dolls, audiotapes, and so forth. The offerings keep getting better and also more ethnically diverse.

Asian-American Curriculum Projects
P.O. Box 1587
San Mateo, CA 94401
Phone: (800) 874-2242
E-mail: *aacpinc@best.com*

This comprehensive catalog of Asian and Asian-American books and educational materials was developed originally by and for educators with the explicit goal of reinforcing and enhancing Asian-American self-image and esteem. The offerings include fiction, biography, cooking, language instruction, academic journals, sociology, politics and history, children's books, dolls, cultural activities (for example, origami, calligraphy, mah-jongg, dragon kites), posters, reference books. There are lots of interesting items for children. The catalog is $3.

Bright Lights Books
8461 South Van Ness Avenue
Inglewood, CA 90305
Phone: (213) 971-1296
Fax: (805) 583-0207
E-mail: *brghtlghts@aol.com*
Web site: *www.brghtlghts.com*

Bright Lights, which is a bricks-and-mortar store as well as an on-line operation, specializes in books for African-American readers of all ages. Its Web site is divided neatly into many age ranges, including infant to three; toddler; and on up. The site also provides information on new books, including long, helpful reviews.

Celebrate the Child
1800 Enterprise Drive, Suite C
Harvey, LA 70058
Phone: weekdays: (888) 223-5278
evenings and weekends:
(800) 237-8400, ext. 34
Fax: (504) 328-7050
E-mail: *Adoptbooks@aol.com*
Web site: *www.celebratechild.com*

Martha Osborne, an adoptive mom (and an adoptee), has done a spectacular job compiling resources across many cul-

tures for adoptive families, and the resources are constantly growing. They include toys and other items (such as "Zoo-sticks," plastic learner chopsticks for children), in addition to books, tapes, and videos. The catalog currently features items on Cambodia, China, India, Korea, Latin America, Russia, Thailand, and Vietnam, as well as more general books on adoption for children and for parents; parenting; travel; cookbooks; and so forth. Osborne also edits *RainbowKids* (see Magazines and Newsletters), an on-line magazine on adoption that explores multicultural issues.
(NOTE: Martha Osborne's family may be relocating to the West Coast as this book is in production. You'll do best to use the Web site for any orders you wish to place.)

China Books and Periodicals
2929 24th Street
San Francisco, CA 94110-4126
Phone: (415) 282-2994
Fax: (415) 282-0994
E-mail: *info@chinabooks.com*
Web site: *www.chinabooks.com*

This wonderful source of books and merchandise about and from China includes not only a full selection of books on Chinese history, literature, language, business, art and culture, and guidebooks but also Chinese music, kites, software (great Chinese clip art), papercuts, maps, and teas. Excellent books are available here on Chinese festivals for children.

Cultural Keepsakes
14 Bruce Drive
South Setauket, NY 11720-1005
Phone: (800) 913-9750
Fax: (631) 588-1931
E-mail: *culturek@erols.com*
Web site: *www.culturalkeepsakes.org*

This resource for families was started in 1989 by Jacqueline Parnell and her Korean-born daughter as a mail-order business. For a print catalog send $2.00 to the address listed here. The Parnells say, "We strongly believe in educating cross-cultural families, and others they come into contact with, about the children's birth culture."

Great Owl Books
41 Watchung Plaza, Suite 112
Montclair, NJ 07042-4111
Phone: (800) 299-3181 or (973) 744-7177
Fax: (973) 893-5900
E-mail: *greatowlbk@aol.com*
Web site: *www./viconet.com/%7Egreatowlbooks/*

Great Owl is a family business that provides fiction and nonfiction books for younger and older children and for adults on a range of topics pertaining to multicultural families. The selection is probably one of the best researched in this area, with a special focus on interracial families known as the "Butternut Collection." I made numerous phone calls requesting a catalog by mail, which I never received, but all the information is on the Web site.

Heritage Key Catalog
6102 East Mescal
Scottsdale, AZ 85254
Phone: (480) 483-3313
Fax: (480) 483-9666
E-mail: *info@heritagekey.com*
Web site: *www.heritagekey.com*

The last time I visited the Heritage Key Web site I was very impressed. The catalog has become very international in scope and lists a lovely assortment of children's books, toys, musical instruments, games, ceramics, and gifts. I saw items from Africa, south and east Asia, much of Europe, and the Americas. The book section is especially helpful, with good summaries of some of the latest titles that are just right for our kids. The catalog features occasional sales on discontinued items at very good prices.

Just for Kids
1822 East Hopi Lane
Mt. Prospect, IL 60056
Phone and Fax: (847) 803-8783
E-mail: *webmaster@just-for-kids.com*
Web site: *www.just-for-kids.com*

This is a mom-and-pop (and kids) operation based in a Chicago suburb. It offers a broad range of children's books, and the multicultural section is quite thorough, with books ranging from African-American and Native American to various foreign language offerings. The selection covers books for infants and toddlers through to young adults, and it includes dictionaries and other types of reference works as well as audiotapes and CDs of favorite stories. Because the company offers 60,000 products and updates its on-line catalog monthly, there is no print catalog.

Just Us Books
356 Glenwood Avenue
East Orange, NJ 07017-3008
Phone: (973) 672-7701
Fax: (973) 677-7570
E-mail: *webmaster@justusbooks.com*
Web site: *www.justusbooks.com*

Cheryl Willis Hudson and Wade Hudson launched Just Us in 1988 as a mom-and-pop outfit publishing books for African-American children. Now their company is the largest of its kind, producing high-quality books with great photos and illustrations. Just Us is known for its Afro-Bets series of books targeting children from two to twelve, and features basic primers on the alphabet and numbers, an Afro-Bets Book Club, and more advanced books on black heroes and African history.

Lectorum
111 Eighth Avenue
New York, NY 10011-5231
Phone: (212) 929-2833 or (800) 345-5946
Fax: (212) 877-LECTORUM
Web site: *www.lectorum.com*

Lectorum offers the most comprehensive catalog I've seen of Spanish-language books, including more than four thousand titles for pre-K through eighth grade. These include translations of English-language classics (*Good Night Moon/Buenas Noches, Luna; The Runaway Bunny/El Conejito Andarín*; and so forth); and other popular books (the *Arthur, Barney*, and *Clifford* series); as well as Spanish originals and some bilingual editions. There are also lots of audiotapes and videotapes of such classics as Tomi Ungerer's *Moon Man (El Hombre de la Luna), Mike Mulligan and the Steam Shovel (Miguel Muligan y Su Pala de Vapor)*, and *Millions of Cats (Millones de Gatos)*.

Lee & Low Books: Multicultural Literature for Children
95 Madison Avenue
New York, NY 10016
Phone: (212) 779-4400
Individual orders: (888) 320-3395
Fax: (212) 683-1894
E-mail: *webmaster@leeandlow.com*
Web site: *www.leeandlow.com*

Although I already owned some Lee & Low Books, I wasn't aware of the company's focus until I stumbled on the catalog at a festival of Asian-Pacific Americans. It's a great resource, and you can order books individually. Specific ethnic categories include African-American, Asian and Asian-American, Native American, and Latino subjects. Some books are in Spanish. There are also "multiethnic books," including some that focus on civil rights, women, single parents, and coping with death. I consider it an exciting catalog and recommend it highly.

Littlechiles.com, INC.
P.O. Box 30326
Palm Beach Gardens, FL 33420-0326
Web site: *www.littlechiles.com*

Littlechiles is an on-line resource providing Spanish-language materials for children.

Multilingual Munchkins
E-mail: *multilingualmunchkin@onelist.com* or *bilingchild@onelist.com*
Web site: *www.multilingualmunchkins.com*

An interesting resource for families trying to maintain more than one language in their home, Multilingual Munchkins' Web site features a newsletter and resources on holiday traditions; foreign language products for children and educators; and collections of songs and recipes from all over the world. Information is drawn from participants. Multilingual Munchkins also maintains a member database that is used to help form playgroups that may be conducted in another language. A related Web site, *www.laukart.de/multisite*, contains songs from all over the world in various languages and is continually expanding.

Pan Asian Publications
29564 Union City Boulevard
Union City, CA 94587
Phone: (510) 475-1185 or (800) 909-8088
Fax: (510) 475-1489
E-mail: *sales@panap.com*
Web site: *www.panap.com*

Launched as a publishing outfit in 1982, Pan Asian Publications is a terrific on-line store offering books in various Asian languages, in English translation, and in bilingual versions. The company has added publications in Spanish and Russian. In 1994 Pan Asian began publishing bilingual (English/Asian languages) children's books and has an excellent section that includes story selections that you can download as a preview before purchasing. My attention was particularly piqued by the listing of a Chinese version of Shel Silverstein's classic *The Giving Tree*.

Redleaf Press
450 North Syndicate, Suite 5
St. Paul, MN 55104
Phone: (800) 423-8309
E-mail: *redleafpress@redleafinstitute.org*

Redleaf Press is a division of Redleaf National Institute, an organization that has been around for many years and that offers support services to family day-care providers. Redleaf recently launched an excellent bilingual (English/Spanish) series called Anti-Bias Books for Kids that targets third- to fourth-grade-level readers, but the books can be read to younger children. (My four-year-old enjoys them.) The children in the stories are of different backgrounds, and at least one character is disabled (as is the case with the main character in a sweet book called *No Fair to Tigers/No Es Justo para los Tigres*). The books also suggest activities for parents and teachers.

2. *Miscellaneous Resources and Series*

Inside Mexico
6750 West Loop South, #500
Bellaire, TX 77401
E-mail: *mexvideo@ragnatela.net.mx*
Web site: *www.inside-mexico.com*

This excellent resource, formed in 1989, provides a range of educational information on Mexican culture. Although its primary mission is to distribute videos, the organization has a terrific Web site that provides information on holidays, stories, recipes, and visual resources. (There was even a special issue of the organization's on-line newsletter focusing on Valentine's Day!) Adoptions from Mexico are relatively few in the overall scheme of cross-cultural adoption, but I think the Web site is an excellent model on how to integrate culture with aspects of daily life.

Of Many Colors: Portraits of Multiracial Families
Gigi Kaeser, photographer, and Peggy Gillespie, interviewer
Family Diversity Projects, Inc.
c/o Chriscomm Management
P.O. Box 1493
Kingston, PA 18704
Phone: (717) 331-3336
Fax: (717) 331-3337
E-mail: *ofmanycolors@familydiv.org*
Web site: *www.familydiv.org*

This book profiles through photos and interviews the lives of thirty-nine families who are biracial through marriage and/or adoption. The traveling exhibit provides the basis for discussions on mixed families. The sponsoring company has a great Web site and has developed media about other areas of family diversity, including gay and lesbian families and families dealing with mental illness.

Ritmo-Y-Mas (Rhythm and More)
Web site:
www.ondanet.com.1995/tejano/tejads/ritmo/ritmo.html

This Web site provides access to a treasure trove of music, literature, and videos focusing on Latino culture. It includes children's literature as well as fiction and nonfiction by Latin American and U.S.-born Latino writers.

Shen's Books and Supplies
8625 Hubbard Road
Auburn, CA 95602
Phone: (800) 456-6660
Fax: (530) 888-6763
E-mail: *info@shens.com*
Web site: *www.shens.com*

Founder Maywan Shen Crach started out as a teacher of English as a second language, and apparently "grew" her business out of a passion. But what a passion! Check out the Web site and you'll see the amazing variety of books she has collected in an amazing array of languages. She is a Cinderella fanatic, so she has unearthed versions of the Cinderella story from around the world. Her Web site also has information on conferences on the West Coast relating to Asian language and educational issues, including some tied to adoption.

3. *Magazines and Newsletters*

Adoption Today
246 South Cleveland Avenue
Loveland, CO 80537
Phone: (888) 663-1186 and (970) 663-1185
Fax: (970) 663-1186
E-mail: *louis@adoptinfo.net*
Web site: *www.adoptinfo.net*

Previously known as *Chosen Child*, this relatively new bimonthly publication (founded in 1998) focuses on international and domestic adoption and foster care issues and is produced by adoptive parents, adoptees, and professionals. A nice feature is the regular contributions by adult adoptees describing their experiences and struggles growing up.

Adoptive Families
New Hope Communications LLC
2472 Broadway
New York, NY 10024
Phone: (800) 372-3300
Fax: (212) 877-9198
E-mail: *info@adoptivefam.com*
Web site: *www.adoptivefam.com*

Adoptive Families, a bimonthly, is a "must" for families who have adopted transculturally (and for any other type of adoption). Its calendar is currently the only centralized listing of adoption conferences, culture days, and heritage camps around the country, with complete contact information. A regular feature is "Growing Up Adopted," which covers age-appropriate milestones.

Interrace
Heritage Publishing Group
P.O. Box 17479
Beverly Hills, CA 90209
Phone: (213) 251-3805
E-mail: *intrace@aol.com*
Web site: *http://members.aol.com/intrace/index.html*

This quarterly magazine examines the concerns of interracial individuals, couples, and families. It features articles on family and social dynamics and has very good information on organizations and Web sites that provide support. The magazine also features cartoons in a series called "Over the Rainbow."

Mavin
1950 Alaskan Way, Suite 123
Seattle, WA 98101
Phone: (888) 776-2846
E-mail: *mavin@aa.net*
Web site: *www.mavin.net*

Mavin is a magazine targeting multiracial young adults, including those born of interracial marriages and those adopted transracially. The entrepreneurial editor/publisher Matt Kelley founded *Mavin* (which comes from the Aramaic and Hebrew words for "One who understands") while he was a freshman at Wesleyan University. As of this writing, he's still an undergrad!

One of the magazine's goals is to link the more than two dozen college-based organizations for mixed-race students across the United States. But the publication appears to be reaching a larger readership of young adults seeking a forum for their specific concerns—and touches on broad issues of culture and identity within the United States and elsewhere. The first two issues had interesting pieces on South Africa and Cuba, for instance, and the third examined cross-cultural adoption.

Multicultural Review
Greenwood Publications
88 Post Road West
Westport, CT 06881
Phone: (203) 223-3571 or (800) 225-5800
Fax: (203) 222-6609
E-mail: *webmaster@greenwood.com*
Web site: *www.mcreview.com*

This quarterly journal targets teachers and may seem too academic for families seeking basic parenting information. It covers a very extensive range of topics. I find it useful as a resource for spotting trends in multicultural education, as well as information on new books, videos, software, and other media. The Web site provides a list of articles, and you can order individual issues.

The Multiracial Activist
Web site: *http://www.multiracial.com*

The Multiracial Activist is a Web journal that is dedicated to the struggle for and preservation of civil rights for multiracial and biracial individuals and interracial couples/families. It also has a very good archive on transracial adoption and excellent book reviews. You can read its e-mail publication, *The Multiracial Activist Newsletter*, for free, but you must sign up to get it. To do so, go to *http://www.multiracial.com/newsletter.html*.

Rainbowkids
Web site: *www.rainbowkids.com*

Martha Osborne, an adoptee and adoptive mother (and the founder of Celebrate the Child, listed under Catalogs and Information Resources), edits this on-line newsletter on international adoption, which features not only articles on all kinds of issues related to adoption but also updated guidelines for adoption from various countries.

Raising Adopted Children
Web site: *www.raisingadoptedchildren.com*

This on-line adoption newsletter is run by Lois Ruskai Melina, an adoptive parent and prolific author of books and print newsletters that address an array of adoption issues. The mother of two grown daughters born in Korea, Melina has extensive knowledge of interracial and multicultural adoption.

Raising Black and Biracial Children
Heritage Publishing Group
P.O. Box 17479
Beverly Hills, CA 90209
Phone: (213) 251-3805

This self-described "journal of color" shares the same publisher and editor with *Interrace* magazine, but the focus is on parenting. (*Interrace* also runs personal ads and features a forum for "couples" issues.) *Raising Black and Biracial Children* covers issues such as racism head-on and includes valuable parenting tips, articles on specific issues concerning racial identity (with frequent references to adoption concerns), and very good references for further reading and research. Although the publication does not aim at adoptive families, I have found some of its articles useful in considering some of the issues my daughter may face as she gets older.

Rethinking Schools
Phone: (800) 669-4192
Web site: *www.rethinkingschools.org*

Rethinking Schools is a provocative journal (with a pronounced left-leaning bent) for educators in the multicultural arena. As a parent and researcher I find it useful, and it has an excellent Web site. The materials are also excellent parent resources.

Roots and Wings
P.O. Box 577
Hackettstown, NJ 07840
Phone: (908) 813-8252
Fax: (908) 813-8201
E-mail: *adoption@interactive.net*
Web site: *www.rootsandwingsmagazine.com* or *www.adopting.org/rw/html*

Cindy Peck, a former teacher who is the single adoptive parent of seven teens and young adults, launched the adoption quarterly *Roots and Wings* more than twenty years ago as a four-page newsletter (initially called *Upcoming*) for adoptive families in her community. *Roots and Wings* addresses a wide spectrum of adoption issues and reaches a global readership. The publication consists predominantly of first-person stories of parents' experiences, although professional commentary is also included. All types of adoption situations are treated in the magazine.

Transcultured
P.O. Box 6037, FDR Station
New York, NY 10050
E-mail: *transcultured@usa.net*
Web site: *www.akaworld.org*

This excellent publication is produced by Also-Known-As, the support organization staffed by adult Korean adoptees. Quite sophisticated in its presentation and depth, the magazine includes many first-person accounts of growing up Korean and some adult observations on identity. *TransCultured* has been invaluable to me in trying to understand the individual experiences and perspectives of adults who were adopted across cultures.

4. Books and Book Series

ANTHOLOGIES, BIBLIOGRAPHIES, AND SOURCEBOOKS

Kruse, Ginny Moore, and Kathleen T. Horning, with Merri V. Lindgren and Katherine Odahowski. *Multicultural Literature for Children and Young Adults: A Selected Listing of Books 1980–1990 by and About People of Color.* Madison, Wisc.: Cooperative Children's Book Center, University of Wisconsin, 1991. This annotated bibliography is an example of an increasing body of multicultural literature resources available for children of all ages, including picture books, activities, poetry, biographies, folklore, and fiction. The appendices identify the authors, illustrators, and the books themselves by ethnic and cultural groups. Recommended resources for further reading and research are included. The center also has a Web site (*www.education.wisc.edu/ccbc/pclist.htm*) that lists small presses owned by people of color specializing in multicultural topics.

Muse, Daphne, ed. *The New Press Guide to Multicultural Resources for Young People.* New York: The New Press, 1997. Funded by the Hitachi Foundation, this tome (and I mean "tome"—it's heavy!) contains more than one thousand critical book reviews organized by general themes—such as family, cultural traditions, ethnic stereotypes, and folk tales—as well as by reading levels. Although the guide targets schools, I find it useful as a personal resource. The reviews are written by teachers, librarians, and other experts in children's education and provide a synopsis of each item. There is also information on multimedia resources, such as CD-ROMs and videotapes, as well as references for people who have special needs and/or speak other languages. Listings include publications in Braille and audio and foreign language materials. Muse, by the way, is also the editor of *Prejudice: Stories About Hate, Ignorance and Transformation* (Hyperion Books for Children, 1998; see under Books for Children).

Weller, Rebecca, ed. *Pact's Book Source: A Reference Guide to Books on Adoption and Race for Adults and Children.* San Francisco: Pact, 1997. Pact is a nonprofit organization that assists with the placement of African-American and multiracial infants with adoptive families. The staff there has produced an extraordinary sourcebook on resources for multicultural families. It covers just about every topic of interest to multicultural families, starting with multicultural board books for infants and including materials for preschoolers, school-age kids, teens and young adults, and adults. Each entry contains a one-line overview of the book, a concise summary of its contents, and a critique. The topics cover a broad spectrum of racial and ethnic identity issues, family concerns, and special needs. Although this sourcebook was previously available only through Pact, I've seen copies at the Barnes and Noble superstore in my neighborhood in New York City. (See also Multicultural Adoption Organizations, Web Sites, and E-mail Discussion Groups in Chapter 8, Goods and Services.)

BOOKS FOR ADULTS

Ethnic Identity

Although books for adult readers on ethnic identity conflicts have been around for years, there is a new generation of books exploring the cultural pressures people face not just as outsiders in a new culture, but as multiethnic individuals trying to find a place for themselves. I've found several contemporary works that touch on identity ambivalence that might benefit multicultural adoptive families, including fiction, essays, and autobiography. Here are a few that have moved me.

Bishoff, Tonya, and Jo Rankin, eds. *Seeds from a Silent Tree: An Anthology by Korean Adoptees.* Glendale, Calif.: Pandal Press, 1997. This is the first collection of poetry, fiction, and personal narratives written by Korean adoptees and exploring issues of adoption, identity, race, and sexuality. Be prepared for some gritty stuff: there's a lot of sadness and bitterness in these texts, reflecting the identity struggles the writers had gone through. It helps to remember that many of the contributors grew up at a time when there wasn't as much support as there is today for cross-cultural adoption, and when some of the writers were the only Asians in their community.

Chiawei O'Hearn, Claudine, ed. *Half & Half: Writers on Growing Up Biracial + Bicultural.* New York: Pantheon Books, 1998. This superb collection of essays draws on writers whose backgrounds range widely, but all represent various ethnic "mixes and matches." (None are from adoptive families, however.) Better-known contributors include *New Yorker* writer Malcolm Gladwell, novelist Gish Jen, and poet Julia Alvarez. The common themes of alienation and trying to fit in pervade the writing, but many of the articles are, in fact, quite funny. They show the ability of the human spirit to transcend prejudice, or at least learn to cope with it.

Cox, Susan Soon-Keum, ed. *Voices from Another Place: A Collection of Works from a Generation Born in Korea and Adopted to Other Countries.* St. Paul, Minn.: Yeong and Yeong Book Co., 1999. In some ways similar to the Bischoff and Rankin anthology previously listed, this collection of writings by Korean adoptees tends to be more diverse in nature, and also more international, since some of the writers grew up outside the United States. I think this work has value to any parent adopting across cultures, and to young adult readers as well. Some of the stories are very emotional, and it is difficult not to be moved by the struggles the writers share with us.

Funderburg, Lise, ed. *Black, White, Other: Biracial Americans Talk About Race and Identity*. New York: Quill Books, an imprint of William Morrow, 1994. Funderburg's interviews with sixty-five biracial men and women, ranging in age from their twenties to their sixties (though most are on the younger side), explore the ambivalence many biracial individuals experience growing up. Adoption does not play a role in this book, but I found many of the stories helpful as I tried to understand what it's like to be different—to look different from most people around you and to come from a family that looks different as well. Many of the families described in the book were broken—the parents had never married or lived together, or they had split up after the children were born. The impact of broken or single-parent families is an issue that some of our kids will contend with.

Jen, Gish. *Mona in the Promised Land*. New York: Knopf, 1996. This funny semiautobiographical book is *not* about adoption, but it does explore some of the identity issues faced by individuals growing up in a culture different from the one their parents knew. In this case, the title character, Mona Chang, is the daughter of upwardly mobile first-generation Chinese parents who have settled in an affluent, mostly Jewish suburb. Gen has also written some pungently funny and ironic essays on the immigrant experience.

Liu, Eric. *The Accidental Asian: Notes of a Native Speaker.* New York: Random House, 1998. This series of essays by a second-generation Chinese-American in his late twenties examines a range of personal identity issues as well as the phenomenon of Asian "success" in the United States. Although Liu doesn't face the dilemma of multiethnic adoptees, he does confront the push-pull between his Chinese roots and his life as a comfortably assimilated Asian-American. Liu makes a sidewise criticism of white families who adopt Chinese children, because he worries about how the children will absorb their heritage. But he's honest in admitting and exploring his own contradictions when he describes his marriage to a white woman and his tentative knowledge of the Chinese language.

McBride, James. *The Color of Water.* New York: Riverhead Books, 1997. This best-seller is a terrific read that focuses on an unusual mother—a white Jewish woman who raised twelve children in the course of marriages to two African-American husbands. Although, like *Black, White, Other*, this book is not an adoption story, I recommend it not only because McBride is a wonderful writer but also because of his insights into what it was like to grow up straddling the different worlds of race and religion and how in adulthood he took a journey into his mother's—and his—past. His mother, Ruth, was born and raised Jewish, but she abandoned her religion and roots when she married McBride's father, an African-American minister with whom she established a church in Brooklyn. When her husband died, Ruth, left with eight children, married again and gave birth to four more children before being widowed a second time. The author's experiences can help us try to see the world through our children's eyes. His mother's emphasis on educating her children despite extraordinary obstacles (she sent all her children to college) comes through with ferocity. At the end of the book, McBride summarizes his siblings' many accomplishments.

Tessler, Richard, Gail Gamache, and Liming Liu. *West Meets East*. New York: Praeger Publishers, 1999. This team of sociologists set out to profile the many families that have embarked on Chinese adoptions during the last decade—especially in the past five years—and conducted a survey of 526 parents, along with some lengthy interviews. Unusual in its scope—this is the first such study on this scale—the book explores who the parents are in terms of age (many are in their forties and fifties), economic status, background, and the ways in which they address the change in their lives brought about through bicultural adoption. It also explores the long-term impact of the age gap between children and parents who are at least forty years older than they are, presenting the possible loss of one or both parents while the child is still relatively young. (Bearing this concern in mind, some parents undertake second adoptions so that their children will not be left alone while still quite young and will have someone with whom to share family memories.)

Parenting

Bartholet, Elizabeth. *Family Bonds: Adoption and the Politics of Parenting*. Boston: Houghton Mifflin Company, 1993. This thoughtful book by a Harvard law professor who is a single adoptive mom describes the author's struggle to adopt from Peru, and analyzes the political and social aspects of international and interracial adoption. Much has changed since Bartholet wrote this book, but certain things have not, including, as she writes, "an enormous amount of process with very little substance." Many families will go through the arduous paperwork and home studies required to adopt without being properly prepared for what it means to be a cross-cultural family.

Hopson, Darleen and Derek. *Raising the Rainbow Generation*. New York: Fireside, 1993. This parenting guide is geared for parents who want to prepare themselves and their children to cope successfully in a multicultural society. It barely touches on adoption, and its emphasis is on African-American families, but some of its strategies should be helpful for people from other backgrounds as well. The appendix features selected folk tales and lists some good resources that were available in the early 1990s when the book was published.

Melina, Lois Ruskai. *Making Sense of Adoption* and *Raising Adopted Children* (revised edition). New York: Harper Perennial Library, 1989 and 1998. Melina provides sage advice for parents seeking to guide their children through the mazes and hurdles of growing up. Her books cover the gamut of adoption issues. I particularly admire her role-playing strategies for helping answer children's (and some adults') questions concerning interracial/cross-cultural adoption. (Example: Child: I'm Filipino, right? Mother: You're Filipino because you were born in the Philippines to Filipino birth parents. You're an American because you are a citizen of the United States. . . .

You can say you are a Filipino-American.) And she's very sharp on how to offer blunt, truthful answers to outsiders' questions.

Pohl, Constance, and Kathy Harris. *Transracial Adoption: Children and Parents Speak.* New York: Franklin Watts, 1992. A short and easy read, this book tells the individual stories of families who have adopted across races and cultures, within the United States and internationally. It also analyzes some of the controversies that have racked domestic transracial adoption (of African-American children by white parents) and discusses some of the important long-range studies examining the impact of cross-cultural adopting. I particularly like the fact that a number of the families profiled adopted children in the 1960s and 1970s, long before there was a critical mass of families doing so. These folks—married and single—were real path breakers for the rest of us. I was heartened by the honesty of the stories. Although the families profiled have dealt with a range of emotional issues, some quite severe, the book projects an ultimately hopeful message that the journeys we're taking are headed to an interesting and gratifying destination.

Register, Cheri. *"Are Those Kids Yours?": American Families with Children Adopted from Other Cultures.* New York: Free Press, 1991. Register's book is a decade old, and the debates about multiculturalism and race within the adoption community have evolved significantly since the time of its publication, but Register covers many bases that are still important to the adoption experience today: How do we tell our children their story? How do we help them explore their roots? How do we promote bonding within our children's new families if they are old enough to have memories of where they came from? Her excellent examples, compassionate writing, and recommended approaches remain very pertinent. I find *"Are Those Kids Yours?"* to be a wise and helpful guide—one of the best around.

Van Gulden, Holly, and Lisa M. Bartels-Rabb. *Real Parents, Real Children: Parenting the Adopted Child.* New York: Crossroad, 1995. This popular and very thorough adoption book covers general adoption issues, starting at infancy, but the emphasis is *not* on interracial or international adoptions, although these topics receive attention. The language is sometimes ponderous and academic—the book tries to be a guide for both professionals and parents, and I don't think this is an easy balance to strike. Still, *Real Families, Real Children* provides an exceptional breakdown of what to expect during stages in our children's development and suggests strategies for answering their questions—or for helping them find answers on their own, in a way that works for them. It has a terrific bibliography. I've heard Holly van Gulden speak, and her passion is almost evangelical.

Watkins, Mary, and Susan Fisher. *Talking with Young Children About Adoption.* New Haven: Yale University Press, 1993. This book sets out imaginary dialogues between parents and children in a variety of situations, including some that specifically address cross-cultural issues.

Wolff, Jana. *Secret Thoughts of an Adoptive Mother.* Kansas City: Andrews McMeel, 1997. Sometimes funny, sometimes cynical, always honest, Jana Wolff describes how she and her husband adopted the infant Ari, of Latino, African-American, and white background. Initially unprepared for transracial adoption, Wolff is now one of the better-known spokespersons on the adoption experience from a parent's point of view, in part because of her willingness to expose her own insecurities in writing. Most of what she deals with, she admits, is about race, and that's something many people don't want to talk about. Finding role models for her son, defending him, creating a strong cultural awareness within the home have all become part of her life as a mother. Wolff also writes for other publications on being part of a multicultural family.

Wright, Marguerite A. *I'm Chocolate, You're Vanilla: Raising Healthy Black and Biracial Children in a Race-Conscious World: A Guide for Parents and Teachers*. San Francisco: Jossey-Bass Publishers, 1998. A little African-American girl with a toothy grin smiles at us from the cover of this book, inviting us in for a refreshing examination of strategies to integrate different cultures into the family and community. One of the key themes that Wright, a clinical psychologist in Oakland, California, explores is that children need consistent positive reinforcement to feel good about who they *are*—and that they should not feel pressure to be someone or something else. She believes strongly that biracial children should be raised with biracial models—and not be coerced into identifying with one race or ethnic group that doesn't honestly reflect their roots. Parents must be strong and firm in building their children's self-confidence and self-esteem from an early age. Since multiracial families these days often include children from Latin American or Asian countries, or other regions of the world different from those of the adoptive parents, I couldn't help thinking that the title should be a bit more inclusive, perhaps adding "and he's butter pecan."

BOOKS FOR CHILDREN

There are so many books on the market, and the choices are growing so fast, that there's no way to provide a comprehensive list here. (You can, however, check some of the anthologies and bibliographies I've listed.) I've assembled a list of books that I particularly like.

It's probably not surprising that a number of them focus on food—what an easy way to bring people of different backgrounds together—and some include recipes. Many are also based on true stories.

Adoff, Arnold. Illustrated by Emily Arnold McCully. *Black Is Brown Is Tan*. New York: HarperTrophy, 1973. This is an adorable and simple celebration of a multiracial family. I was surprised to discover that this classic gem has been around since the early 1970s. (Where was I?) It's a story-poem that draws a bit on baby talk and simple language to profile a loving family. Here's a sample: "There is granny white and granny black/kissing both your cheeks and hugging back."

Carling, Amelia Lau. *Mama and Papa Have a Store*. New York: Dial Books for Young Readers/Penguin Putnam, 1998. This lovely book recalls Carling's childhood in Guatemala City, where her Chinese-born parents ran a fabric store that also sold soy sauce and other Chinese goods, firecrackers, and toys. Many of the customers were Mayan weavers who bought colorful Chinese silk threads for the fabrics they wove. Carling herself "weaves" local lore into this story, with some of the Chinese customs that her family retained in their adopted country. The visual evocation of life in Guatemala is stunning. (Carling now lives and works in the United States.)

Cisneros, Sandra. *Hairs Pelitos.* New York: Dragonfly Books/ Alfred A. Knopf, 1997. This bilingual book, with great pictures by Terry Ybanez, describes the different way hair looks in one Mexican family.

Commissiong, Wilesse A. F. *The Best Face of All.* Chicago: African American Images, 1997. The author, an African-American educator, wrote this book when her daughter was a preschooler as a way to provide positive images for her child at a time when there were few books to highlight the physical varieties among black children.

Dooley, Norah. Illustrated by Peter Thornton. *Everybody Cooks Rice.* Minneapolis: Carolrhoda Books, 1991. Carrie's little brother, Anthony, has wandered away from home just before dinner, and Mom asks her to find him. Visiting neighbors on their street, Carrie finds that Anthony has stopped by neighbors from Barbados, China, India, Puerto Rico, Vietnam, and so on. At each house she sees (and sometimes tastes) the various rice dishes the family prepares. By the time she returns home, Anthony is already there, feeding baby sister Anna, and Mom is preparing an Italian rice dish her grandmother used to cook. The story takes a delicious approach to promoting diversity—and includes recipes children can prepare with their parents' help. An excellent companion book by the same author is *Everyone Bakes Bread* (Minneapolis: Carolrhoda Books, 1996), which includes recipes for Indian chapatis, Barbadian coconut bread, and corn bread, among others.

Fox, Mem. Illustrated by Leslie Staub. *Whoever You Are.* San Diego: Harcourt Brace, 1997. This is one of the first picture books I bought for my daughter. Its beauty is its magical depiction of children and lands of different colors, looks, and landscapes that come across as natural and easy. The language is very simple, talking about how we all laugh, cry, love, learn, and ache in similar ways, no matter who we are, where we live, or what we aim to do with our lives. The illustrations are perfect.

Freeman Ellis, Veronica. Illustrated by George Ford. *Afro-Bets' First Book About Africa: An Introduction for Young Readers.* Orange, N.J.: Just Us Books, 1989. This primer on Africa for young children provides a great foundation on African history. I was wondering how anyone would tell the story of Africa in such a short space, but this book does it very well through clear prose, great illustrations, and terrific photos. The Afro-Bets Kids—a regular feature of the Just Us series—lead us into the story, and young readers learn about early African kingdoms, the history of the slave trade, Africa's ecology, apartheid in South Africa, Africa's artistic and cultural traditions, and so forth. It's the best book I've seen for introducing Africa to young children (of at least age six).

Hamilton, Virginia. *Bluish.* New York: Blue Sky Press, 1999. Hamilton is a veteran writer of young adult novels that examine racial issues. In this one, for readers aged nine to twelve, "Bluish" is the nickname given to a new girl at school, wheelchair-bound because of recent leukemia treatments, and having a somewhat translucent, "bluish" skin as a result. In fact, she is biracial, and her mixed background is also a source of interest to the main character, Dreenie, who is black and becomes one of Bluish's new friends.

Hausherr, Rosmarie. *Celebrating Families*. New York: Scholastic Press, 1997. This seems like a simple book: each two-page spread features a color photo on the left-hand page with images of the child's parents (or grandparents) and other key family members, and the right-hand page shows a black-and-white photo of a family activity. The text, usually one or two short paragraphs, summarizes the family experiences. The wonderful thing about this book is its inclusivity, richness, and very positive tone. There are foster families, single-parent families, gay and lesbian households, biracial families, stepfamilies, extended families, and one family headed by a grandmother. There's even a profile of a homeless family and of a little boy whose father is currently in prison. I found the family tree discussion on the last page to be a bit troubling since adoptive families, and a number of the other models in this book, are built from a different template. (See The Challenge of Family Trees in Chapter 4.) Still, I highly recommend this book for its wonderful images and wide-ranging portrayal of what families look like.

Katz, Karen. *The Colors of Us*. New York: Henry Holt, 1999. This book describes the search by a little girl named Lena for the right colors to paint pictures of her friends. She realizes that they come in all different shades of brown—coffee, peanut butter, chocolate, and so on. It's a simple read, but an enjoyable example of the lovely work of Karen Katz.

Katz, Karen. *Over the Moon.* New York: Henry Holt, 1997. This book, a favorite of my daughter, describes a couple's journey to adopt a little girl in another country far away. The couple is clearly Caucasian, the daughter darker-skinned, and the story is a blissful telling of how the couple's dream of a family is realized through their journey. I also appreciate the book's honesty in describing the mother who couldn't care for the little girl. Katz's adoptive daughter was born in Guatemala.

Kurtz, Jane. *Faraway Home.* San Diego: Harcourt Brace, 2000. Although born in the United States, Jane Kurtz grew up in Ethiopia and has written several books for young adults that evoke life there. Some are idyllic—she lived there before the famine—but she has also recently tackled some more difficult aspects of life in Ethiopia, particularly in her 1998 book, *The Storyteller's Beads* (Gulliver Books), which describes the plight of two girls who must flee their towns because of war. In *Faraway Home*, an African-American girl named Desta deals with her father's imminent departure for Ethiopia, where he is from, to tend to his elderly mother. As he prepares his daughter for his time away, he tells her stories of what Ethiopia was like.

Lee, Marie G. *If It Hadn't Been for Yoon Jun.* New York: Avon, 1995. One of very few adoption-themed novels for young readers that I have found, Lee's book focuses on Alice, who was adopted from Korea as an infant and is now an "all-American" girl, fully assimilated into her community. When a young Korean student named Yoon Jun arrives at her school, Alice is asked to be Yoon Jun's "buddy" to help the newcomer adapt. Embarrassed for being singled out, Alice then confronts identity issues that she had suppressed, about what it means to be Asian, to look different, and to have a different background. It's a nice book—and an important one.

Mandelbaum, Pili. *You Be Me/I'll Be You.* Brooklyn, N.Y., and La Jolla, Calif.: Kane/Miller Book Publishers, 1990. Originally published in French, with the title (in translation) *Black Like Coffee, White Like the Moon,* this charming book describes what happens when a biracial girl tells her Caucasian father that she doesn't like the way she looks because she isn't white, like him. In response, he puts on brown makeup and lets his daughter braid his hair, while he powders her face with flour and she puts on his hat, and the two go out for a stroll. Gentle discussions between them about racial perceptions ensue. Of course, people react strangely at the sight, but the little girl's black mother, whom they meet on their way, scolds the "two clowns" and tells them to go take a shower! In the end, the little girl asks her mother what you get when "a piece of moon falls into a cup of coffee?" The answer? "You get me!"

Muse, Daphne, ed. *Prejudice: Stories About Hate, Ignorance and Transformation.* New York: Hyperion Books for Children, 1998. This collection of fifteen stories targets young adults (junior and senior high school) and includes authors as diverse as Flannery O'Connor, Sandra Cisneros, and Ntozake

Shange. Not specifically about adoption—or even multicultural issues—the book examines various ways that young people can experience prejudice. I'm comfortable including it in this list as a way of helping our children become more conscious of how different people (and writers) experience prejudice.

Namioka, Lensey. *Yang the Third and Her Impossible Family.* New York: Yearling, 1995. Mary (Yingmei) Yang tells the hilarious story of her family's attempts to adapt to American culture and make friends during their first year in Seattle—and of their American-born neighbors' attempts to understand the Yangs, who maintain many Chinese customs. One of four children of immigrants from Shanghai, Mary grapples with American holidays (the book opens as the Yangs prepare for their first Thanksgiving), etiquette (it's *not* a compliment to tell an adult she looks older than her age), and customs (such as the oddity of dog-sitting). Mary, meanwhile, learns that her new friends are convinced that she *eats* dogs. While not an adoption story, the book is a great introduction for young readers to multicultural issues and can be particularly instructive to families considering adopting older children. (It's fun for adult readers, too.) There are three other titles about the Yangs: *Yang the Youngest and His Terrible Ear* (New York: Yearling, 1994), *Yang the Second and Her Secret Admirers* (New York: Little, Brown, 1998), and *Yang the Eldest and His Odd Jobs* (New York: Little, Brown, 2000).

Petertyl, Mary. *Seeds of Love: For Brothers and Sisters of International Adoption.* Grand Rapids, Mich.: Folio One Publishers, 1997. Petertyl's book, loosely based on her own experiences, tells the story of how the parents of a little girl (through birth) prepare her for the arrival of a sibling, who will be adopted internationally. The book, targeted for younger readers, thus tackles both the issue of how an only child adapts to losing her status, and how a family becomes multicultural.

Rattigan, Jama Kim. Illustrated by Lillian Hsu-Flanders. *Dumpling Soup*. Boston: Little, Brown, 1993. Set in Hawaii, this autobiographical book tells the story of Marisa, who helps her Korean-born grandmother prepare New Year's dumplings for the first time. But the story is really about growing up in a multicultural Hawaiian family. There's a glossary of words in Korean, Chinese, and Japanese—and a recipe for dumpling soup.

San Souci, Robert. *Sukey and the Mermaid.* New York: Aladdin Books, 1996. This is a retelling of an African-American folk tale about a girl named Sukey who runs away from a hard-driving stepfather and finds solace with Mama Jo, a brown-skinned mermaid. Each day Mama Jo gives Sukey a gold coin; every day her stepfather spends the money on himself. The story, which weaves in the folklore of South Carolina and West Africa, explores how Sukey eventually finds freedom. The drawings are by Brian Pinkney, one of my favorite illustrators of books on African-American themes.

Say, Allen. *Allison*. Boston: Houghton Mifflin Company, 1997. I love Allen Say's books and have read many of them to my daughter—but not *Allison* (yet). It's a difficult story, depicting a young Asian girl, adopted by white parents, who becomes aware that she is different from her parents when her grandmother sends her a kimono. This awareness, compounded by her discomfort with being adopted and knowing nothing of her birth parents or country, sends her into a rage, and she destroys some of her parents' favorite objects. A stray cat becomes her companion—she soon "adopts" it—and the meaning of adoption and the potential it offers for profound love becomes clear to her through her relationship with the cat. The artwork is beautiful, but I wonder why, in this story, anyway, the parents kept their daughter's story from her, causing so much distress. Do we read this book to our kids, or enjoy Say's other great works? I own the book, but I haven't decided yet! Those parents who've been honest about adoption from the very beginning should not have to encounter Allison's type of rage. Perhaps the book is a good lesson on what *not* to do when we adopt cross-culturally.

Senisi, Ellen B. *For My Family, Love Allie.* Morton Grove, Ill.: Albert Whitman & Co., 1998. In this wonderful book, with photographs taken by the author, a young biracial girl describes the preparations for a large gathering of relatives on both sides of her family, and how she prepared a big platter of peanut butter treats. By rolling some in white coconut flakes, others in brown cocoa powder, and leaving the rest plain, she creates treats in many colors—like the members of her family. Yes, a recipe is included!

Vinje, Marie. Illustrated by Gail L. Suess. *Hanna's Butterfly.* Grand Haven, Mich.: School Zone Publishing Co., 1992.

This book is part of the Discovery Zone readers series, and the story has nothing to do with multicultural issues. But, as illustrated, the daughter is clearly Asian and the mother is Caucasian. This is one of the few examples I've found—aside from the works of Vera Williams and Helen Oxenbury—that features a multiracial family just as a coincidence.

Williams, Vera. *"More, More, More," Said the Baby.* New York: Mulberry Books, 1996. This book for very young children tells three lovely stories about family love. The images show, without having to spell it out, families that are clearly of different races, and that's the beauty of this particular book. It made me a fan of Williams, whose other delightful books depict families of different racial and economic backgrounds, often in an urban setting. Several of the stories focus on working-class families, and some of the families are headed by single mothers. Williams has kept a core group of readers in mind with her down-to-earth, affectionate books such as *A Chair for My Mother* and *Cherries and Cherry Pits.*

Wing, Natasha. Illustrated by Robert Casilla. *Jalapeño Bagels.* New York: Atheneum Books for Young Readers, 1996. In this book, Pablo tells the story of how he fulfilled a class assignment to bring something from his culture to school. Since Pablo's father is Jewish and his mother is Mexican—and since they run a Jewish-Mexican bakery—he figures he'll bring in something from there. The book takes us through Pablo's experiences helping his parents bake. He makes *empanadas de calabaz* (pumpkin turnovers) and delicious *chango* rolls and helps his father knead and shape bagels. Ultimately he decides to bring jalapeño bagels to school because, he says, "they are a mixture of both of you. Just like me!" It's a lovely book—with recipes at the end. The theme is certainly relevant to what many of us try to do in creating multicultural homes.

MULTICULTURAL ACTIVITIES AND CELEBRATIONS

Multicultural Activity Books

Kohl, Mary Ann F., and Jean Potter. *Global Art: Activities, Projects and Inventions from Around the World.* Beltsville, Md.: Gryphon House, 1998. This book contains dozens of crafts projects from around the world (including Antarctica), and each is rated on the experience needed (one to three stars), the art techniques required (painting, sculpture, collage, and so forth), and the amount of planning and preparation (the lowest, 1, means all materials can probably be found around the house; the highest, 3, would require purchasing some materials at art supply shops or hardware stores). Each activity has a "Did you know?" box that offers tidbits of historical and cultural information on the people or region represented.

Milord, Susan. *Hands Around the World: 365 Creative Ways to Build Cultural Awareness and Global Respect.* Charlotte, Vt.: Williamson Publishing Company, 1992. This book offers a range of activities—crafts, recipes, songs, games, and so on—that aim to build cultural awareness among children. The book also lists organizations, suppliers, and related titles.

Pooley, Sarah. *Jump the World: Stories, Poems and Things to Make and Do from Around the World.* New York: Dutton Children's Books, 1997. This charming book includes stories, proverbs, recipes, poems, and crafts that are packaged in a colorful, witty book with great illustrations. Among all the books I've listed here, this one works best as both a nighttime storybook *and* an activity book, and I like the variety.

Terzian, Alexandra. *The Kids' Multicultural Art Book: Art and Craft Experiences from Around the World.* Charlotte, Vt.: Williamson Publishing Company, 1993. This book provides instructions for art projects adapted from around the world. The projects are easy to do and clearly explained and illustrated step-by-step. Examples include Korean dragon puppets, Chinese egg painting, African mud cloth designs, and Mexican paper flowers. Materials are basic—you can find most of them at home—and the projects don't make too much mess. The book includes a bibliography.

Celebrations

Bernhard, Emery. Illustrated by Durga Bernhard. *Happy New Year!* New York: Lodestar, 1996. This lovely book explores the different New Year celebrations around the world, focusing on such common features as noisemakers and then looking at specific customs, and ways that people say good-bye to the year that has passed. (In Colombia, people put an egg in a glass of water and watch how it changes to try to see things that will happen in the year to come.)

Jones, Lynda. *Kids Around the World Celebrate!: The Best Feasts and Festivals from Many Lands.* New York: John Wiley and Sons, 2000. This delightful book offers a combination of anecdotes, craft projects, and recipes to make sixteen holidays the world over accessible to children. Jones divides the holidays into four groups: New Year's celebrations (China, Ecuador, Scotland, and the United States), fast days (such as Brazil's Carnival and New Orleans's Mardi Gras, and festivals in Saudi Arabia and Venice, Italy), Thanksgiving (Barbados, India, Nigeria, and the United States), and a category she calls "Renewing the Spirit": Israel (Chanukah), Japan, Mexico, and the United States (Kwanzaa). The illustrations are easy to follow, and many instructions wisely begin, "Ask an adult to help you . . ."

Kindersley, Barnabas and Anabel. *Children Just Like Me: Celebrations! Festivals, Carnivals and Feast Days from Around the World.* New York: DK Publishing, 1997. This elaborately designed book includes gorgeous photographs and tons of information about seasonal holidays around the world, including, for instance, how children celebrate birthdays. It's a cross between a coffee-table book and a reference book. Its pages are so "busy" with pictures and bits of text that they may be confusing to children.

Stepanchuk, Carol. *Red Eggs and Dragon Boats: Celebrating Chinese Festivals.* Berkeley, Calif.: Pacific View Press, 1994. Stepanchuk provides detailed history, explanations, stories, activities, and recipes related to five key Chinese holidays: the Lunar New Year, Clear Brightness Festival,

Full-Month Red Egg and Ginger Party, Dragon Boat Festival, and the Moon Festival. Traditional Chinese folk paintings and paper cuts serve as many of the illustrations.

BOOK SERIES

Festivals of the World
Gareth Stevens Publishers
P.O. Box 56
Hubertus, WI 53033-0056
Phone: (414) 225-0333
Fax: (414) 225-0377
E-mail: *info@gsinc.com*
Web site: *www.gsinc.com*

Gareth Stevens publishes the extensive Festivals of the World series, which, at my latest count, included thirty-six books on festivals in different countries worldwide. Beautifully produced, these books contain color photos and many crafts and recipes, along with a history and description of the traditions of the countries profiled. This series is recommended for children six and older. Each is thirty-two pages with hardcover library binding—and a bit steep at about $20 each. (I've seen different prices on various Web sites and in catalogs. Individual books are available in Asia for Kids and some of the other catalogs listed at the beginning of this chapter.)

Legends of the World
Troll Associates
Troll Communications, LLC
2 Lethbridge Plaza
Mahwah, NJ 07430

Phone: (888) 998-7655
Fax: (888) 718-7655
E-mail: *Webmaster@troll.com*
Web site: *www.troll.com*

This series of inexpensive paperbacks ($3.95–$4.95) retells traditional legends of various countries. Examples include *Juan Bobo and the Horse of Seven Colors* (Puerto Rico), *Child of the Sun* (Cuba), *Finast the Falcon* (Russia), and *The Golden Slipper* (Vietnam). I've also seen Japanese, Ghanaian, and Latvian books in the series. There are also Spanish-language versions of some stories and two subseries: Legends of the Americas (titles from Argentina, Brazil, Guatemala, and Mexico, among others) and ten books of African legends that comprise the African Legends Reading Centers. Some of these books are available in kits with teaching manuals and audiotapes to listen to as you read along with the text. The illustrations are lovely, and each book contains one page of background about the country of origin, including history and current conditions, and some discussion of the tale that has been retold. Although Troll sells in bookstores, much of its distribution is to schools and through book clubs. The Web site does not list all the available titles, so you should request a catalog at *www.troll.com/school/catalog.html*. Indicate that you are making the request as a parent rather than as an educator.

Let's-Read-and-Find-Out Science Books
HarperTrophy/HarperCollins Books
10 East 53rd Street
New York, NY 10022

This series is *not* about multiculturalism, but about various science topics geared to younger readers. What I like about these books—besides the fact that the topics themselves are explained clearly and easily so that my young daughter understands them—is that the images of children are multiracial, include a good gender balance, and also depict children who are disabled.

A World of Difference
Children's Press
Grolier Books
90 Sherman Turnpike
Danbury, CT 06816
Phone: (203) 797-3500 or (800) 353-3140
Fax: (203) 797-3197
Web site: *www.grolier.com*

This is a series of glossy, thirty-two-page paperbacks on specific topics such as toys, dolls, hats, food, hair, masks, and other common items, with each book describing what the items look like and how they're used around the world. The books, with titles such as *What a Doll!*; *Hair, There and Everywhere*; and *Let's Eat* are profusely illustrated with gorgeous photographs, and there is plenty of information. My two criticisms—and this, of course, is an adult point of view—are that the material seems chaotic, and there's no hands-on activity (a recipe or an easy craft) to enable the reader to become part of what he or she is reading. There's so much going on, and although the types of toys or other items described are grouped into topics (*Toys Everywhere* has sections on different types of balls, toys made from recycled materials, and toys associated with religious beliefs), I would be curious to know how children respond to the presentation. But overall the books are terrific—or I wouldn't mention them here—and the paperback versions retail at just $6.95. Each book has a good table of contents, glossary, and index.

eight

Goods and Services

1. Toys
2. Greeting Cards, Calendars, Visual Arts, and Gift Items
3. Food: Ingredients, Cookbooks, and So Forth
4. Multicultural Adoption Organizations, Web Sites, and E-mail Discussion Groups
   - Country-Specific and Ethnic Adoption Web Sites and Listservs
   - International Adoption Resources (General)
5. Culture Camps
   - General Culture Camps (Multicultural)
   - Country-Specific and Ethnic Culture Camps
6. Homeland Trips

1. Toys

This list represents a selection of companies that provide multicultural dolls and toys suitable for multicultural adoptive families. You should also consult the catalogs listed in Chapter 7, Publications; many are expanding their inventory to include dolls, toys, and games.

Apple Tree Dolls and Bears
401 East Front Street
Port Angeles, WA 98362
Phone: (888) 452-3021
E-mail: *info@dollsnbears.com*
Web site: *www.dollsnbears.com*

Merrily and Ted Ripley, who also run the Adoption Advocates International agency, created their business partly so they could locate dolls appropriate for their own diverse family, which includes three birth children and eighteen adopted children from many backgrounds. Their company now offers a lovely (and pricey) selection of collectible dolls and bears, including many ethnic dolls: African-American, Asian, South Asian, Hispanic-American, South American, Native American, and South Sea Island. The costumes and features of the dolls are quite elaborate.

Childswork/Childsplay
135 Dupont Street
P.O. Box 760
Plainview, NY 11803-0760
Phone: (800) 962-1141
Fax: (516) 349-5521
Web site: *www.childswork.com*

This company's products target a range of social and emotional needs of children and adolescents and can be used by therapists, educators, and parents. You'll see materials that aim to help "angry" children understand their feelings, and others related to attention issues, stress, and fears. Adoption is just one category covered here, but there are lots of relevant toys, including Multi-Ethnic "Flexible" Caucasian, African-American, Hispanic, and Asian Families. (My one regret is that you have to buy a "whole" family of each race, and you cannot request, for instance, a Caucasian mother and an Asian daughter!) There are also puppets, board games, and posters.

Global Friends Dolls
Phone: (800) 393-5421
Fax: (415) 513-4066

Global Friends Dolls are for girls eight and older and include special accessories, adventure books, a range of outfits, videos, and furniture (such as a futon for the Japanese doll). The countries represented range from Egypt to Kenya to Japan to China to regions of the United States. At this writing, the easiest way to access local dealers in Global Friends Dolls was from different e-stores on the Internet, including *eToys.com* (the following Web site was under construction: *www.globalfriends.com*).

Kaori's Kids
E-mail: *2ndgrade@worldnet.att.net*
Web site: *www.baddog.com/Asiandolls/*

Kaori Brown began selling her handcrafted twenty-six-inch rag dolls while she and her husband were awaiting the referral and arrival of a child from Korea; proceeds from the sales of the dolls helped pay for the adoption. The Browns eventually became the parents of a boy, Jae-Sun. Brown's dolls are quite elaborate, and she will make them to your specifications. A custom doll is about $75.

Live and Learn
P.O. Box 498
Reisterstown, MD 21136
Phone: (443) 394-8501
E-mail: *toys@liveandlearn.com*
Web site: *www.liveandlearn.com*

This interesting Web site offers an array of parenting materials as well as on-line activities for children (coloring books, games, picture books) and, at this time, a modest selection of multicultural dolls, mainly Asian and African-American. There are also several wooden kits made by artisans from Chile and Bolivia, which a child (five or older) can assemble and paint: a rain stick, a Bolivian flute, and carved animals. This is a Web site only.

Multicultural Kids
P.O. Box 757
Palatine, IL 60078-0757
Phone and Fax: (847) 991-2919
Phone (orders): (800) 711-2321
Web site: *www.multiculturalkids.com*

This company offers a range of books, videos, arts and crafts materials, puzzles, music cassettes, dolls, and various other collectibles and ornaments from around the world. Nancy Moody, the adoptive mom of two children from China, set up Multicultural Kids in 1997 so she could work at home, and she has done a classy job of including many types of ethnic groups and families within her offerings. Materials are available on lots of cultures, including African-American, Chinese, Hispanic, Indian, Jewish, Native American, Vietnamese, and Russian. She also has specific categories, including parenting and single-parent families. This is a Web site only.

My Twinn
The Lifelike Company
3231 South Platte River Drive
Englewood, CO 80110
Phone: (800) 469-8946
E-mail: *webmail@mytwinn.com*
Web site: *www.mytwinn.com*

This company creates twenty-three-inch-tall dolls that look like your child, based on a personal profile and photos that you submit. (And if the doll you receive doesn't look enough like your child, you can send it back to the "Doll Hospital.") These dolls are expensive—$119.95 for non-poseable dolls and $139.95 for poseable models—but families I know who've bought them are pleased. You can request them for ages three to twelve and select outfits from the company's catalog. There may be an extra charge if your child wears many braids, and you cannot pierce the doll's ears or request dimples, but My Twinn designers will add freckles, birthmarks, and moles. My Twinn also has a few noncustomized multicultural dolls, babies, and a new line of brother and sister dolls.

2. *Greeting Cards, Calendars, Visual Arts, and Gift Items*

Most mainstream card companies depict families that are unlike ours (though even greeting cards are changing). Therefore, some enterprising adoptive families, or people who work with them, have established businesses to create and market products for us.

AdoptShoppe.com

Owned by Roberta Rosenberg, author of *Adopting from Korea: A Parent's Guide to Korean Adoption*, AdoptShoppe offers books, fabric arts, jewelry, adoption journals, and other adoption gift items. A nice product is the Memory Book gift basket for families who are preparing to adopt.

ASHA, Inc. (Americans Support Heritage for Adoptees)
65925 61st Street
Bend, OR 97701-8701
Phone: (541) 385-0746
Web site: *www.deschutes.net/India/*

This very interesting Web site offers an array of toys, music, clothing, packaged food, jewelry, books, and other items from India. Some of the crafts are made by organizations that work in disadvantaged communities in India.

ChinaSprout.com
663 Carroll Street
Brooklyn, NY 11215
Phone and Fax: (718) 789-3662
E-mail: *xiaoning@chinasprout.com*
Web site: *www.chinasprout.com*

This adoption dot-com is perhaps one of the more entrepreneurial sites I have run into. Founder Xiaoning Wang, a Chinese national living in Brooklyn, New York, has formed a comprehensive Web site offering products, as well as activities and information, targeting families who have adopted from China. She also publishes a monthly on-line newsletter that describes Chinese holidays and rituals, with recipes and related information.

Chinesefolkart.com
(formerly Xinde Jia—New Family Kids' Services)

This Web-based venture offers products and services for families who have adopted or are planning to adopt from China, with an emphasis on Chinese folk art. Peasant paintings, commemorative stamps, note cards, batik designs, jewelry, greeting cards, calendars, and other items are available. The company, run by Steven Hardy, an adoptive parent, and Xiao Yi, who has helped facilitate adoptions in Jiangxi Province, also offers a translation service and a "China information desk" for families.

Colorful Families Greeting Cards
P.O. Box 893
Duluth, GA 30096
E-mail: *sales@colorfulfamilies.com*
Web site: *www.colorfulfamilies.com*

An adoptive parent created this line of personalized greeting cards when she realized there were none for her particular family. You can skim through the Web site and select designs and greetings according to your needs. There are cards for single-parent families. You can choose holiday or seasonal settings and a range of ethnicities. The company is gradually expanding its product line.

FamilyCulture.com
The FamilyCulture
166 Oak Street
Ashland, MA 01721
Phone: (508) 881-7156 or (888) 261-5188
Web site: *www.FamilyCulture.com*

This Web site originated in 1995 as a newsletter by Bet Key Wong, an Asian-American mother, for Asian-American families. It became a dot-com in 1997, selling products with an emphasis on Asia. I have noticed Mexican and African-American dolls among its series of multicultural dolls, which come with your choice of different outfits. But that product line is limited. The Web site also has some very interesting articles on raising children cross-culturally, mostly first-person accounts.

Good Orient Enterprise
Web site: *www@viaweb.com/goodorient/index.html.*

This cyber retailer offers numerous Chinese items including silk *cheongsams* (Hong Kong–style dresses), kids' Chinese clothing and pajamas, paintings, Chinese horoscope greeting cards, and so forth.

HeartandSeoul.com
E-mail: *heartandseoul@home.com*
Web site: *www.HeartandSeoul.com*

This company is typical of a growing number of home-based enterprises started by adoptive families seeking either to earn money while raising their children or, in some cases, to raise funds to pay for an adoption. As the name of the business implies, Linda Crawford and her husband adopted from Korea, and the products focus on Korean themes: Barbie *hanboks* (Korean doll gowns), Korean cookbooks, and so forth. But the site offers other interesting international items and projects, such as "toothpick flags," in which families can download images of flags from the country their children come from and create decorations on toothpicks. The Web site also features Korean and Chinese recipes and a page of products offered by other adoptive families as well as a "mini-mall" of goods and services offered by families seeking to raise additional funds so that they can adopt.

International Mission of Hope—Vietnam
Web site: *www.imh-vn.org/gifts.htm*

This Web site is sponsored by an organization that provides funds and material support to families in Vietnam, and it includes an array of gifts, books, and other items for purchase. Profits go toward humanitarian projects.

Madeinthephilippines.com
Ad Infinitum
3940 West Cornelia
Chicago, IL 60618
Phone: (773) 539-0596
E-mail: *flip@madeinthephilippines.com*
Web site: *www.madeinthephilippines.com*

This is a lovely place to find products of all types from the Philippines.

Miracle of Adoption
P.O. Box 12408
Cincinnati, OH 45212
Phone: (800) 741-0711
Web site: *www.miracleofadoption.com*

This company, formed in 1995 by Gail Huff, an adoptive mother, and her sister, Brenda, who is also an adoptive parent, produces custom-made cards, candy bar wrappers, prints, T-shirts, and caps with the Celebrate Adoption logo, and other products for adoptive families. You can e-mail a description or send a photo and they'll build a design around it. The Web site gives samples of the company's artwork and messages.

Multiculturalcalendar.com
Web site: *www.multiculturalcalendar.com*

This Web site exists solely to market a multicultural calendar that lists the cultural festivals of several dozen countries and the religious festivals of twelve major religions.

Namaste.com
Web site: *www.namaste.com*

This on-line resource specializes in books, music, food, and recipes from India. It's a fun site, owned by *ethnicgrocer.com*. (See below.)

Rodina Treasures
10440 Windsor Park Drive
Alpharetta, GA 30022
Phone: (770) 619-3019
Fax: (770) 752-9264
E-mail: *TotRodina@aol.com*
Web site: *www.rodinatreasures.com*

This Web site specializes in selling crafts from Russia, including traditional wooden stacking dolls, icons, painted eggs, and lacquer boxes.

3. *Food: Ingredients, Cookbooks, and So Forth*

Emasala.com
Web site: *www.emasala.com*

This on-line retailer will ship all the ingredients required for South Asian cooking—and recipes, too.

Ethnicgrocer.com
Web site: *www.ethnicgrocer.com*

This site will help you find all sorts of ingredients for ethnic cooking and will explain how they are used. The site has diversified into books, music, recipes, and multimedia for individual ethnic groups.

Frieda's
Web site: *www.friedas.com*

This company has helped popularize fruits and vegetables from outside the United States, including those commonly used in Asian and other ethnic cooking: the Web site has lots of recipes. Frieda's can mail-order gift baskets.

Global Food Market
Web site: *www.globalfoodmarket.com*

This site offers spices and gift baskets from Asia, Spain, Italy, Israel, and India.

4. *Multicultural Adoption Organizations, Web Sites, and E-mail Discussion Groups*

The Internet enables families to collect extensive information on adoption more quickly and comprehensively than ever. For multicultural families, I highly recommend the following five Web sites for general and specific information.

Evan B. Donaldson Adoption Institute
120 Wall Street, 20th Floor
New York, NY 10005
Phone: (212) 269-5080
Fax: (212) 269-1962
E-mail: *info@adoptioninstitute.org*
Web site: *www.adoptioninstitute.org*

Founded in 1997, the Evan B. Donaldson Adoption Institute has already made a mark as a preeminent research, policy, and advocacy organization involved in promoting adoption awareness, maintaining up-to-date databases on adoption, running surveys (including the Benchmark Survey mentioned in Chapter 1), and developing adoption training curricula. A current key focus is ethics in adoption.

National Adoption Information Clearinghouse
33 C Street, SW
Washington, DC 20447
Phone: (703) 352-3488 or (888) 251-0075
Fax: (703) 385-3206
E-mail: *naic@calib.com*
Web site: *www.calib.com/naic*

Established in 1987 as a service of the Children's Bureau within the Department of Health and Human Services, the NAIC provides outstanding information resources on almost every adoption issue, including international and interracial adoption. Much of the information is free, although there is a charge for some publications. The Web site also lists conferences, adoption links, and culture camp programs around the United States.

New York State Citizens' Coalition for Children, Inc.
306 East State Street, Suite 220
Ithaca, NY 14850
Phone: (607) 272-0034
E-mail: *office@nysccc.org*
Web site: *www.nysccc.org*

This outstanding Web site is valuable for adoptive families of all types, offering extensive resource materials on transracial adoption, including an excellent archive of articles by parents and adoptees on their experiences growing up. The organization offers a great twenty-minute video, *Struggle for Identity Issues in Transracial Adoption*, in which transracial adoptees and their families discuss their struggles with racism, search for identity, and efforts to create a sense of place. For price and ordering information, contact NYSCCC or PhotoSynthesis Productions at 418 North Tioga Street, Ithaca, NY 14850, phone: (607) 272-4242.

Pact, An Adoption Alliance
1700 Montgomery Street, Suite 111
San Francisco, CA 94111
Phone: (415) 221-6957
Fax: (510) 482-2089
E-mail: *info@pactadopt.org*
Web site: *www.pactadopt.org*

Founded in 1991, Pact is a nonprofit organization that provides educational events and services for birth parents, adoptive families, and adopted children, with an emphasis on transracial adoption. Although not an adoption agency, Pact has worked with facilitators to help with adoption placements. The Web site provides articles, books, links, and a listserv to communicate with birth parents, adopted people, adoptive parents, and adoption professionals.

TransRacial Adoption Group
32 19th Avenue, Suite 100
Los Angeles, CA 90291-4113
Phone and Fax: (310) 289-2127
E-mail: *info@transracial-adoption.org*
Web site: *www.transracial-adoption.org*

The TransRacial Adoption Group is a national nonprofit founded in 1996 as a research institute to exchange information on domestic and international transracial adoption worldwide. Its offerings include support groups, legal aid and advice, and, more broadly, suggestions on how to advocate for nondiscriminatory adoption practices. Its four areas of focus are public awareness, client support, research, and litigation.

COUNTRY-SPECIFIC AND ETHNIC ADOPTION WEB SITES AND LISTSERVS

There are many discussion groups for families who have adopted cross-racially or internationally. Some of these are country-specific, while others look at such specific concerns as racial identity and adoption of older or special needs children. New discussion groups are being created all the time since all that's required is for one person (you, for instance) to sign on with one of the many servers that host these discussions and then get the word out to other lists (also called "listservs").

I've been a member of the Post-Adopt-China (PAC) list for some years. It was formed when the general list for families who were planning to adopt from China and the families who had already done so got too big, and it became apparent that the needs of the two groups were distinctly different. Then, during 1999, two new lists were spun off, one for families who had adopted older children from China or were thinking of doing so (*aok-china@egroups.com*) and another on issues relating to raising older children who had been adopted from China, whether the children had been adopted as infants or as older children (*RaisingChinaChildren@egroups.com*).

Some on-line companies host their own discussion sites. America Online has an extensive adoption program including many lists on specific adoption topics. Type the keyword *Adoption* and you'll get there. *About.com* also sponsors many adoption discussions, including an excellent resource on transracial adoption at *adoption.about.com/parenting/adoption/cs/transracial/index.htm.*

Egroups.com hosts many adoption discussions. Also many adoption agencies now have their own Web sites, some quite sophisticated, and they are becoming more so over time. A few agencies host their own discussions, which are open to anyone who is interested. (Some examples are listed below.) Find these sites by searching under "Adoption Agencies."

INTERNATIONAL ADOPTION RESOURCES (GENERAL)

African Adoption

PLAN (in Oregon) and MAPS (in Maine) handle adoptions from the few countries in Africa that have adoption programs; there may be others not listed here.
Web site: *www.egroups.com/community/africanadopt*

This Web site is for families, adoptees, and anyone else interested in African adoption issues.

African-American Adoption

Web site: *www.adopting.com/Xculture*

Although this listserv addresses cross-cultural adoptions in general, much of the discussion that I've followed addresses adoptions of African-American children by African-American parents. It's a very animated and interesting discussion group.

Brazilian Adoption

Web site: *www.limiar.com*

LIMIAR is the best-known agency handling adoptions in Brazil. Founded in 1981, it's a nonprofit that works directly with Brazilian courts and orphanages, publishes a quarterly English-language newsletter, and sells products of interest to families created through Brazilian adoption. The organization also hosts Back-to-Brazil trips for Brazilian teens and parents, as well as an annual LIMIAR Family Reunion (east and west coasts) attended by families throughout the United States, Canada, and other countries.

Cambodian Adoption

Web site: *www.egroups.com/subscribe/CambodianAdoptions*

This site provides information to prospective and current parents of children adopted from Cambodia.

Chinese Adoption

Families with Children from China
Web site: *www.fwcc.com*

Families with Children from China is the most comprehensive Chinese adoption Web site, and provides links to related sites. On offer here are extensive cultural coverage, adoption guidelines (with updated information on adoption regulations in China), membership networks, and a "mall" that describes books and services for families. *Chinasprout.com* markets educational products and gifts, targeting families who have adopted from China. (See under Greeting Cards, Calendars, Visual Arts, and Gift Items.)

East European Adoption

Web site: *www.eeadopt.org*

This Web site provides general information on Eastern European adoption and specific information on adoption in Bulgaria, Belarus, Russia, Romania, Hungary, Ukraine, and Georgia—and also Kazakhstan in Asia. You can use this Web site to get subscription information on listservs focusing on these countries. The Web site has been updated and is now quite comprehensive, including thorough adoption information as well as books, toys, and other resources for the home. This site has created various listservs to discuss Eastern European adoption.

SEEA-L (Singles Eastern European Adoption List)
This is a listserv for single parents who have adopted from Eastern Europe. For information, check *www.eeadopt.org* or send an e-mail to *help@eeadopt.org*.

Ethiopian Adoption

African Cradle, Inc.
509 13th Street, Suite 5
Modesto, CA 95354
Phone: (209) 575-1980
Fax: (209) 575-1982
E-mail: *info@africancradle.com*
Web site: *www.africancradle.com*

African Cradle is an unusual adoption agency in that it not only focuses on only one country—Ethiopia—but it is also involved in activities to promote Ethiopian culture, so that families adopting children with the agency have access to extensive resources. Amber Stime-Kassa, who was adopted from Ethiopia as a youth, founded the agency in 1992 and works directly with one children's home in Ethiopia. The Web site has a terrific selection of links, and lists children's books on Africa and organizations that promote Ethiopian culture.

Guatemalan Adoption

A general list is Guatemala-adopt, and you can subscribe by contacting *listserv@maelstrom.stjohns.edu* and then typing "subscribe Guatemala-Adopt Firstname Lastname" (without quotes—and using your own real first name and last name). A second list for older children adopted from Guatemala is part of the egroups listservs. The information e-mail address is *olderkidsguatemala@onelist.com*.

Indian/South Asian Adoption

iChild
Web site: *www.serve.com/ichild*

The iChild Web site is an outstanding resource for information about all aspects of Indian and Indian subcontinent adoption (Nepal, Pakistan, Sri Lanka, Bangladesh, and others). It includes information on iChild chapters throughout the United States; cultural programs; charitable initiatives in the subcontinent; resources for books, music, and related products from India; and a new group for families of Indian background who have adopted from India. The site also hosts chat groups.

Kazakhstan Adoption

Web site: *www.littlemiracles.org*

This discussion is sponsored by an adoption agency that handles many Kazakh adoptions. You may also want to check *egroups.com* to find out if new Kazakh adoption discussion groups have been formed. A group of parents is forming a "PAKK" group—Parents of Kazakh Kids.

Korean Adoption

Probably the two best-known Web sites on Korean adoption are those formed by Also-Known-As and Holt International Children's Services. Both Web sites are very comprehensive. Adopt Korea is owned by Kaori Brown, an adoptive parent.

Here are three Web sites to try out: *www.akaworld.org*, *www.holtintl.org*, and *www.adoptkorea.com*.

Latin American Adoption

Latin American Parents Association (LAPA)
P.O. Box 340-339
Brooklyn, NY 11234
Phone: (718) 236-8689 (information line only)
Web site: *www.lapa.com*

LAPA is an umbrella organization for all types of Latin American adoptions, and it provides current information on adoption guidelines in Brazil, Chile, Colombia, and Guatemala as well as links to adoption programs elsewhere in the region. Membership includes a subscription to the newsletter *Que Tal*? The Web site gives information on conferences and also features some great recipes.

Paraguayan Adoption

Web site: *www.pyadopt.org*

This impressive Web site lists an array of Paraguayan cultural activities and information about its nationwide chapters. It not only promotes networking on Paraguayan adoption but also links members to organizations doing humanitarian work in Paraguay. You can download the Paraguayan national anthem from this site.

Parents of International Children

Web site: *www.parentsofintchildren.com*

The Web site title is a bit misleading, because most of the organizations the site represents are Asian (lots of Korean, and some Chinese and Vietnamese). This Web site has a good links page that will direct you to a range of adoption resources, including gifts, photolistings of waiting children, and on-line resources.

Romanian Adoption

Web site: *www.eeadopt.org*

As with some of the other Eastern European adoption sites, access to a listserv on Romanian adoptions comes through the umbrella Web site *www.eeadopt.org*. You can register directly by sending an e-mail to *ReqRL@eeadopt.org* and type in the message: "subscribe Romania-list Firstname Lastname."

Russian and Ukrainian Adoption

Web site: *www.frua.org*

Families for Russian and Ukrainian Adoption provides general information on adoption from Russia and Ukraine. The toys and books section is actually a link to *eToys* and *Amazon.com* and does not focus on products from Russia or Ukraine.

Thailand Adoption

Web site: *www.egroups.com/subscribe/Thailandadopt*

This Web site is moderated by Martha Osborne, who also publishes the international adoption Webzine *RainbowKids.com*.

Vietnamese Adoption

Adoptive Parents of Vietnam
Web site: *www.comeunity.com*

Families with Children from Vietnam
Web site: *www.fcvn.org*

Adoption from Vietnam is relatively new, but listservs by and for families who have adopted there or are planning to are already quite active.

5. Culture Camps

Culture camps can be daylong, weekend, or even weeklong programs. For the most part, these camps consist of recreational and cultural activities geared to the particular ethnic background of the participating children and their families. Activities range widely and often include language workshops, songs, sports, puppet shows, trying on clothing, ethnic cooking and eating, art and drama projects, and presentations of plays, music, and videos from the home country/culture. Many culture camps have parallel programs for parents and encourage sibling participation whether or not the sibling shares the adopted child's background. The parents' programs may include workshops on raising children from another culture and discussions on specific issues.

Currently, the most up-to-date and comprehensive single print resource for information is *Adoptive Families* magazine, and the best on-line resources I have found are on the Web site of the National Adoption Information Clearinghouse (*www.calib.com/naic*). You can also find out about camps by checking individual agency Web sites and inquiring in adoption discussion groups. America Online lists culture camps as a discussion category in its adoption site.

There is no single database (yet) of adoption-related culture camps, and new camps are being created regularly. Some are privately owned, others are sponsored by agencies, and most are nonprofit.

Here's a sampling of culture camps.

GENERAL CULTURE CAMPS (MULTICULTURAL)

Colorado Heritage Camps, Inc.
Attention: Pam Sweetser
2052 Elm Street
Denver, CO 80207
Phone: (303) 388-3930
Fax: (303) 388-2909
E-mail: *hcamps@juno.com*
Web site: *www.heritagecamps.org*

At present, Colorado Heritage Camps program is the largest and most comprehensive culture camp program I know of, and its programs are branching out into many areas of ethnic and interracial adoption. Current programs include African-American, East Indian, Chinese, Korean, Latin American, Vietnamese, Filipino, and Russian culture for adoptive families.

An excellent feature of the Heritage Camps Web site is the cultural links for each of its programs.

Hands Around the World (HATW)
Gail Walton
1417 East Miner Street
Arlington Heights, IL 60004
Phone: (847) 255-8309
E-mail: *HANDSATW@aol.com*
Web site: *communities.chicago.digitalcity.com/CP/homepage/1,1677,T-2195,00.html*

One of the nicest things about HATW, which was launched in 1987, is that its family camp programs bring cultures together—eight different cultures were listed in the organization's Web site. A five-day program takes place at a site north of Chicago for African-American children and children from South Asia, Korea, Latin America, Eastern Europe, the Philippines, and China.

Although HATW originally recruited area families, it now accommodates out-of-town participants. Director Gail Walton also edits *Connections*, a newsletter for families with children from South Asia. The camp is always held the last full week in July, with programs running from 9:30 a.m. to 3 p.m. Children of dual heritage may arrange to take part in specific activities at different camp programs based on their backgrounds. A nice aspect of holding all the programs during the same week is that the food menu rotates, and everyone has the opportunity to try different ethnic meals: one day is Korean, the next South Asian, and so on.

Holt International Children Services
Culture Camp Programs
P.O. Box 2880
Eugene, OR 97402
Phone: (541) 687-2202 (ask for Todd Kwapisz)
E-mail: *info@holtintl.org*
Web site: *www.holtintl.org/camp.html*

Holt was one of the originators of Korean adoption in the 1950s. It sponsors camps around the United States, not restricted to Korean culture. Programs include art, music, language, crafts and games, and sports activities. You do not have to be a Holt client to participate.

COUNTRY-SPECIFIC AND ETHNIC CULTURE CAMPS

Chinese Culture Camps

In addition to a program sponsored by Colorado Heritage Camps (see above), new Chinese culture camp programs have sprung up around the country, including Camp China, a "sister" program to Colorado's China camp that's based in Black Mountain, North Carolina, and uses a similar structure. Deb Luppino, an adoptive mother, has compiled a Web site of these camps, which she periodically updates. You can access it at *members.home.net/dluppino/Culture/Camps/Culture/home.htm.*

Maine China Culture Camp
Peter or Meg Kassen
Hidden Valley Camp
Freedom, ME 04941
Phone: (800) 922-6737
Fax: (207) 342-5685
E-mail: *chinakids@hiddenvalleycamp.com*

This camp has been around for a while. For one weekend in late August, Meg and Peter Kassen convert Hidden Valley Camp, a "regular" sleepaway camp they own, into a China culture camp after the regular season ends.

Filipino Culture Camps

Camp Mabuhay
Contacts: Carol Dispoto at (973) 398-1020 or Debra Hartman at *djh@eqsystems.com*

The Filipino adoption community in the mid-Atlantic region sponsors an annual weekend culture program in Columbia, Maryland, each July. A Filipino school in Washington, D.C., assists with programs. The parent coordinators change each year, but you can find them by contacting the individuals listed here.

Indian/Indian Subcontinent Culture Camps

Supportive Parents and Indian Children Everywhere
(SPICE)
Christine Futia
1 Marjaleen Drive
Randolph, NJ 07869
E-mail: *CFUTIA@aol.com*
Web site: Check *www.ichild.org* for updated site information or contact Ms. Futia.

SPICE hosts a family heritage camp for families whose children were born in India, Nepal, Pakistan, Sri Lanka, and Bangladesh, that is held at a different retreat center each year, generally in the mid-Atlantic region. A SPICE store offers books, bindis, jewelry, stationery, incense, dolls, clothing, and other South Asian items. Sales proceeds support indigent families in India, and the children write letters to these families as part of their heritage camp activities.

Korean Culture Camps

The following list was assembled by Also-Known-As and details on each camp vary; you can contact the camps directly for specifics.

Camp Hwarang Teen Camp
Minneapolis/St. Paul, MN
Phone: (612) 644-3251 (Yoon Ju Park)

Camp Moo Hung Hwa
3311 Forest Grove Court
Durham, NC 27703
Phone: (919) 596-5112 (Beth Van Dyne)
E-mail: *jacobmolly@aol.com*

Camp Moon-Hwa
815 Ninth Street, SW
Rochester, MN 55902
Phone: (507) 281-5838 (ask for Deb Resman)
Web site: *members.aol.com/MoonHwa/*

Camp Mujigae Korean Culture Day Camp
Parsons's Child and Family Center
60 Academy Road
Albany, NY 12208
Phone: (518) 426-2600 (Cathy Sutton)
Web site: *www.crisny.org/not-for-profit/mujigae/*

Camp Sae Jong
P.O. Box 250632
Franklin, MI 48026
Phone: (248) 851-7314
E-mail: *saejong@aol.com*
Web site: *www.sequoianet.com/saejong*

Camp Sejong
79 South Street
Demarest, NJ 07627-2411
Phone: (201) 784-1081
E-mail: *lgelber@msn.com*
Web site: *sejong.linkage.org*

Kamp Kimchee
7081 Schley Road, SE
Brainerd, MN 56401
E-mail: *jackson@brainerd.net*
Web site: *www.kampkimchee.org*

Korean Culture Camp
Minnehaha Academy
North Campus, Minneapolis, MN
Phone: (612) 866-9039 (ask for Jean McCabe)

Pride in Our Heritage Camp
Vienna, VA
Phone: (202) 726-7193 (Eunice Park)

The Korea Society
Attention: Gretchen Sampsen
950 Third Avenue, 8th Floor
New York, NY 10022
Phone: (212) 759-7525
Fax: (212) 759-7530
E-mail: *korea.ny@koreasociety.org*

UNESCO International Youth Camp (IYC, UNESCO Youth Center, I'chon, South Korea) is sponsored by the Korean National Commission for UNESCO, in conjunction with The Korea Society. Activities focus on issues relating to human rights, environment, and cultural heritage. Campers will work toward meeting the IYC's founding goals of promoting international understanding, inspiring respect for human dignity, and encouraging development of enlightened work ethics. Campers must pay for round-trip airfare between the United States and Seoul and for incidental expenses; expenses in Korea (program, lodging, food, and local transportation) are covered by the Korean National Commission for UNESCO; camp participation fees are covered by The Korea Society. For people ages eighteen through twenty-four.

Latin American Culture Camps

Mi Pueblo Culture Camp
William Gruber
2714 Leighton Road
Shaker Heights, OH 44120
Phone: (216) 371-3570
E-mail: GruberWL@aol.com
Web site: *www.concernforchildren.org*

Mi Pueblo Latin American Culture Camp is sponsored by Concern for Children, Inc., a not-for-profit adoption support group in Cleveland. Since 1993, a four-day culture camp program has been in place for children adopted from Latin

America and their siblings. Bill Gruber, who chairs and directs the camp, notes that about eighty-five children from kindergarten through eighth grade take part each year, along with fifteen teen volunteers, many of whom are adoptees (and former campers), and parents. There is also day care. The camp is operated by volunteers, except for four teachers hired from Cleveland's Latino community. Most campers come from Ohio and Michigan, but some have come from Wisconsin, Maryland, Indiana, New York, Pennsylvania, and other states.

During camp week, the children have daily classes in Spanish, Latino culture, games, crafts, dance, and music. Special presentations include animal exhibits, puppet shows, modern dance and Flamenco performances, and a band. Role models from the Latino community, such as a college president and a physician, give presentations. Each year has a different theme, such as the Olympics, ancient civilizations, World Cup soccer, Latinos in the United States, and so forth. Authentic Latin American lunches are served each day.

Romanian Culture Camps

"Celebrate Romania" Weekend (Minnesota)
Mike Francis
Phone: (320) 532-3767 or (800) 822-0152

A family retreat for families with children from Romania.

6. *Homeland Trips*

The Ties Program
11801 Woodland Circle
Hales Corners, WI 53130
Phone: (800) 398-3676
Fax: (414) 774-6743
E-mail: *info@adoptivefamilytravel.com*
Web site: *www.adoptivefamilytravel.com*

The Ties Program organizes family "homeland" tours to the birth countries of adopted children. Current tours include Korea, Peru, Paraguay, and Chile; new tours are scheduled for China and Guatemala, with plans eventually to arrange tours to Romania. Tours are guided by someone who knows the country well. The Korean tours have been led by Deborah Johnson, who was adopted from Korea and is well known in the international adoption community for her insights on identity issues that our children may confront. Johnson is on staff at the organization.

acknowledgments

Dozens of families and individuals took time to describe their experiences and recommend materials that have helped them create homes appropriate to their multicultural needs. Some requested anonymity. Others are mentioned by name in the book, and I'm grateful for their generosity. They are too numerous to mention here, and I'm afraid to leave anyone out, but I would like to acknowledge their invaluable support.

I want to extend special thanks to Hollee A. McGinnis (a.k.a. Lee Hwa Young), founder of Also-Known-As, and Joy Kim Lieberthal, who shared some of their experiences of being adopted and have also become important "movers and shakers" in promoting youth leadership in the adoption community. Cheri Register, the author of *"Are Those Kids Yours?"*—one of the best books on identity questions related to cross-cultural adoptive families—allowed me to interview her at great length and provided some important baseline insights as I proceeded with the book. Lascelles Black, a family therapist in Mount Vernon, New York, served as a sounding board when I was just beginning the book, and shared some important thoughts with me that I've included in the text.

My participation in a number of e-mail discussion groups also provided a great foundation for ideas and contacts. Quite a few participants and some of the resources I've listed in Part II originated in these discussions. Theresa and Bill McLean have done a prodigious job maintaining e-mail discussion groups for parents of children born in China. I also wish to thank Beth Waggenstack, Beth Peterson Kruger, and Maria Valentas, who helped me contact adoptive families on discussions lists to which I do not belong. These families have adopted children from Russia, Eastern Europe, India, and Latin America. Sue and Hector Badeau provided invaluable insights on all aspects of multicultural parenting—and their family is an inspiring model.

My editor, Elisabeth Kallick Dyssegaard, prodded me into a careful and focused development and vision of the book and made many wise and discreet suggestions on how to move it forward. Robyn Creswell and Rahel Lerner, also at Farrar, Straus and Giroux, gently offered cheerful encouragement and insights. Helen Carr copyedited the manuscript with great sensitivity. My agent, Gareth Esersky, understands me and has helped me interpret ideas into proposals that work.

My family—parents and siblings—support me with their admiration and abiding encouragement. But none of this would be possible without my daughter, Sadie, for whom there are not enough adjectives in English (or Mandarin, or any other language) to sufficiently express my love.